"A well-written, insightful resource offering hope and power to those challenged by the presence of a depressed parent. *Children of the Depressed* provides readers with the ability to understand and overcome a difficult period. More importantly, it offers a road map to the healing process."

> —**Linda O'Connor**, freelance writer and host of *Parent Talk*, a weekly parenting radio show on Timeless FM 102.9 and AM 1230 WECK in Buffalo, NY

"As children, few of us understood the lasting impact that living with a depressed parent would have on our lives. Shoshana S. Bennett demystifies this phenomenon in an easy to understand book that provides not only the understanding of what children experience, but practical steps that lead to lifelong healing."

> —**Patricia de Lambert, RN, BS, MA**

"*Children of the Depressed* should be required reading for everyone! Shoshana S. Bennett has created a concise, clearly written, and inspirational guidebook. I could relate personally, since my father was bipolar and I was also depressed while raising my children. Thank you, Dr. Shosh, for this unique and timely book."

> —**Jane Honikman, MS**, cofounder of Postpartum Education for Parents and founder of Postpartum Support International

"Shoshana S. Bennett intimately understands depression and offers other children of depressed parents enlightened ways of getting to a better place. Combine that with insight, practical exercises, and clear therapeutic processes, and you have a book that feels as though it was written while gently holding a child of depressed parents in her loving arms."

—**Suzi Snyder, PhD**, lifelong learner and educator who looks to transform lives through a combination of life coaching, Eden Energy Medicine, and ancient feng shui principles

"Lovingly drawing from her personal and clinical experience, [Bennett's book] is a gift to everyone who has had a depressed parent. Shoshana S. Bennett shows how a depressed parent may affect you and how you can heal. Whether you are sixteen or 106—if you think you had or have a depressed parent, this common-sense book can change your life and relationships!"

—**Bruce Linton, PhD**, director of the Fathers' Forum and the author of *Becoming a Dad: How Fatherhood Changes Men*

"This book is a must-read for adults who grew up with a depressed parent. Shoshana S. Bennett provides easy-to-understand information and offers realistic hope. The book is filled with practical tools to promote healing."

—**Barbara Grelling, PhD**, clinical psychologist in private practice specializing in the treatment of women with perinatal depression and anxiety

"*Children of the Depressed* provides a compassionate, honest, and thoughtful guide for adults who are on a journey of healing the wounds of their childhood. Through stories, clinical research, and experience, Shoshana S. Bennett offers sage advice on how to understand and overcome the consequences of living with a depressed parent. She shines a bright light on the path to living a full and meaningful life. I know many people will be deeply grateful for this book."

> —**Rona Renner, RN**, temperament counselor,
> parenting coach, and author of *Is That Me Yelling?*

"Brilliantly written by the renowned clinical psychologist, Shoshana S. Bennett, *Children of the Depressed* offers help and hope to those who grew up with a depressed parent. Powerful and inspirational, this book provides eye-opening explanations, real-life examples, and concrete solutions on how to achieve a more meaningful and fulfilling life despite the challenges of childhood."

> —**Svetlana Blitshteyn, MD**, director and founder of
> Amherst Neurology and Dysautonomia Clinic and
> coauthor of *POTS: Together We Stand*

Children

of the

Depressed

Healing the Childhood Wounds That Come from Growing Up with a Depressed Parent

Shoshana S. Bennett, PhD

New Harbinger Publications, Inc.

Publisher's Note

This publication is designed to provide accurate and authoritative information in regard to the subject matter covered. It is sold with the understanding that the publisher is not engaged in rendering psychological, financial, legal, or other professional services. If expert assistance or counseling is needed, the services of a competent professional should be sought.

Distributed in Canada by Raincoast Books

Copyright © 2014 by Shoshana S. Bennett
New Harbinger Publications, Inc.
5674 Shattuck Avenue
Oakland, CA 94609
www.newharbinger.com

Cover design by Amy Shoup
Acquired by Jess O'Brien
Edited by Brady Kahn

Library of Congress Cataloging-in-Publication Data on file

FSC
www.fsc.org
MIX
Paper from
responsible sources
FSC® C011935

Printed in the United States of America

16   15   14

10   9   8   7   6   5   4   3   2   1   First printing

Contents

Foreword

As a primary care pediatrician, I am often corrected when I refer to the parents of the children in my practice as "my patients." Strictly speaking, they are not. Unlike a family physician, I don't check their blood pressure or cholesterol or listen for heart murmurs in their chests. But the health of the children in my practice is directly related to the health and behaviors of their parents. Cigarette smoking is an obvious example. Secondhand and thirdhand smoke affects the health of children in many ways. What is less obvious are the effects of modeling. Having a parent who smokes makes it twice as likely that you will begin smoking as a teenager. Whether consciously or unconsciously, we are constantly modeling behavior and attitudes for our children.

In the course of my day, I interview and examine children while talking to them about healthy habits and behaviors. I spend just as much effort interviewing parents, trying to get a sense of their personal challenges as parents and what resources they have to help them along this important journey. A depressed parent is part of a child's family history, the list of diagnoses and conditions that are more likely because of their genetic makeup. A depressed parent also becomes an important part of the social history, things that affect a child directly or indirectly: family support, living situation, socioeconomic class, education, pets, environmental exposures, and parental employment. A depressed parent has a hard time caring for his or her family—this is no secret. How children experience this affects their childhood, their adulthood, and their own parenting.

Scientists of varied disciplines have taught us a great deal about the mind over the past twenty years. Using advanced techniques and research methods, we now know that the brain is not static—there is growth and change throughout much of our lives. Neuroplasticity, epigenetics, toxic stress, cortical remapping, critical period of brain development, neurogenesis, and DNA methylation are all terms that have become part of our scientific vocabulary. While the past imprints on us and influences our future, there is no doubt that we humans are capable of great change and can understand, overcome, and redirect the course of our lives. Our current biology is not our destiny, nor are we a sum total of our genetics and experiences. There are variables and mutations not yet understood—all of which we can modify and in some way control.

Children of the Depressed represents hope and power. Those readers whose early years and critical periods were challenged by the presence of a depressed parent will gain the hope that they can understand and overcome this difficult period, and the power to begin the healing process. I have had parents in my office, describing a difficult situation in their own childhood, who have said, "It stops here. It stops with me." This book helps make that statement a reality. Understanding what has been imprinted in your genes and your psyche by a depressed parent is the first step toward overcoming it. This is how you help yourself and your family. *Children of the Depressed* will help you examine the past, learn from your experiences, understand how they influence you even now, and then look forward with strength and resolve. Most of all, I think this book will give you hope, and that hope will be the fuel for your journey.

—Nelson Branco, MD, FAAP
Tamalpais Pediatrics
Greenbrae, CA

Acknowledgments

A few days after signing the contract with New Harbinger Publications, I was diagnosed with breast cancer. Without the support of my colleagues Margie, Jordan, and David, I could not have delivered this book in the timely manner required.

Joe and Tyler, your candid feedback was much appreciated. Laura Hulka, thank you for your research help.

A special thank you to acquisitions editor Jess O'Brien, who inquired about my interest in authoring *Children of the Depressed*. To editorial manager Jess Beebe, project manager Jesse Burson, editor Brady Kahn, assistant editor Vicraj Gill, production manager Michele Waters, typesetter Tracy Carlson, proofreader Gloria Sturzenacker, and art director Amy Shoup, thank you all so much for your respective talents.

To the many wonderful children of depressed parents I interviewed and have worked with over the years, I am very grateful for your honesty, forthrightness, and insight. You are all examples of the joy that is possible after moving through the tough times.

—Shoshana S. Bennett, PhD

Introduction

No one wants to be depressed or to be directly touched by depression. Not you. Not your parents or caregivers. And not your siblings or children, if you have any. None of us wants depression in our lives. Depression is awful. It stinks in every way. There is no romance, no fun, and no joy in depression.

While grief—and some degree of psychological suffering—is a normal part of life that none of us can completely escape, depression is something quite different. Depression is more than a bit of a thief. It can rob us, taking the wind right out of our sails, the air right out of our lungs, and the meaning right out of our lives. At least, that's how it feels at the time. It can even take away our parents.

If you have one or more parents (or caregivers) who have suffered from depression, you know what I'm talking about. If your mom or dad suffered or suffers from depression, it may feel like you didn't, or still don't, really have your mom or dad present as a parent. Why? Because it is hard to have parents if depression has them instead. They don't belong to you. They belong to their depression.

HOW THIS BOOK WILL HELP

While there are numerous books detailing what it is like to suffer from depression, there has never before been a book written directly for the children of the depressed. This book answers certain questions: What kinds of situations tend to arise for children of the depressed? How can you come to terms with having a depressed parent? Are there certain skills that may prove helpful? Conversely, are there certain ways that you learned to cope as a child that may be defeating you now and thwarting your happiness as an adult? And if you have your own children, what can you do to make sure that you greatly limit—or better yet, completely eliminate—the passing on of any harmful behavior patterns?

The good news is that now, more than ever before, there is hope for the depressed and the children of the depressed. While depression can be a silent assassin, killing joy in the family, it is not a life sentence for either the depressed person or that person's children.

What's most important for you to know now is that depression is not a death sentence. For instance, one of the more effective methods for treating depression—cognitive behavioral therapy (CBT)—has been a lifesaver for many. In a nutshell, CBT is a way of examining the role that our thoughts (or cognitions) and behaviors play in determining the quality of our lives—or lack thereof. CBT offers a variety of methods to help us challenge and change certain thoughts, feelings, and behaviors that are causing difficulties so that we can improve the quality of our lives and, more specifically, the quality of our relationships. These same methods can help you, the child of a depressed parent, improve your life and relationships.

You can go from seeing depression as a way of life to seeing depression as a chapter in your life. Perhaps it is only an early chapter. Put differently, what happened early in your life need not determine the middle and ending of your story. You can create a new story line, with the real possibility of your life being even richer and more rewarding because of what you have experienced and overcome.

So, if there is or was a depressed parent or caregiver in your life, and...

- If your life seems to have become a major weight that you shoulder with as much nobility as you can muster, then this book is for you

- If that extra weight makes even daily chores into a burden—the kinds of things that under normal circumstances would be a breeze—then this book is for you

- If you are barely able to imagine a different way of being, then this book is for you

In short, if you are ready to become fully healthy, and if you are willing to try something different that stands a very good chance of working, then this book is for you.

WHY I WROTE THIS BOOK

While I am indeed someone with a doctorate in clinical psychology who successfully treats many clients, I am not *just* a licensed and practicing therapist. Far from it. I grew up the child of a brilliant and amazing—but periodically depressed and anxious—father. So perhaps not unlike you, I have experienced the weight of parental depression.

In addition, I myself have worn the foggy, distorted lenses of depression while tending to my duties as a mother. With two severe postpartum depressions and no existing professional help, I did not always tend to those tasks all that well. With tremendous guilt and helplessness, I witnessed the effects that my illness was having on my beautiful son and daughter. I have also witnessed the remarkable healing of us all, separately and together. I know it is possible. I have lived it and have since helped thousands of families do the same.

My work as a therapist began with my experience as a depressed mother. When I realized what a lack of effective information and outreach there was for mothers suffering from depression, I knew I'd found my life's calling. Only then did I change careers and train to become a licensed therapist. My previous books, *Beyond the Blues, Postpartum Depression for Dummies,* and *Pregnant on Prozac,* came out of both my own experience with depression and my work as a therapist helping others.

So please trust that for me the topic of depression is not some cold clinical term, one that I use to describe the experiences of other people. Therapy, for me, is personal. And so, too, is this book.

WHAT YOU CAN EXPECT

What I hope you will find here is a map out of the often flooded lowlands of being a child of the depressed. In essence, what this book offers is a guide to higher ground. If you are not sure if you are a child of the depressed or otherwise might benefit from this book, chapters 1 and 2 offer some user-friendly assessments to help you sort things out. Importantly, you don't need to be the child of a parent who received a clinical diagnosis of depression for this book to be of service to you. It may have been something as simple as your mother or father experiencing a loss that they never seemed to recover from—be it a death in the family, a debilitating physical ailment, divorce, or loss of a home or job.

Chapter 1 will have you explore whether your parent was depressed as you were growing up. What might that experience have been like and felt like to you? This chapter will include an exercise to help you consider the severity of your parent's depression.

Chapter 2 is where you will explore the relationships within your family and the impact that depression in the family may have had on these relationships. It will look at the family as a whole and how depression could have affected your relationships with siblings (if you have any) and your parents' relationship with each other.

Chapter 3 will look at what I have come to view as the basis of all healing, which is support and encouragement. After all, without lots of support and encouragement, how can you begin anything as challenging as examining the role that your parent's depression had in your life? Chapter 3 will also look at a few obstacles to healing that may come up.

Chapter 4 will take you into the realm of your thoughts and inner narratives, introducing the idea that we each have voices that live inside us and tell us stories about ourselves. This chapter will help you ponder the possibility that the less helpful of these voices and their stories may come from your past experience as the child of a depressed parent and will encourage you to tell yourself more supportive (and truthful) stories about yourself and your life. This chapter will include a brief introduction to cognitive behavioral therapy and its benefits in treating depression. It also contains a profound exercise, derived in part from CBT principles, that will help you heal your emotional and psychological wounds.

Chapter 5 will further explore the realm of your feelings, which are closely related to your thoughts and patterns of thinking. It will explore the emotional challenges that may continue to haunt your adulthood because your parent was not emotionally available as you were growing up, and give you some new tools for re-parenting yourself to ease the pain of difficult emotions and to allow you to embrace the full range of human experience.

Chapter 6 is all about the B in CBT: the behavior element. What we do—or, conversely, don't do—has an impact on the quality of our lives. This chapter will look at some of the more common behavioral traits that children of the depressed exhibit and will help you look at your own behaviors so that you can begin to change any that are problematic.

Chapter 7 is an in-depth look at the difficulties that children of the depressed may have in maintaining healthy boundaries in relationships. It will teach you how to create better boundaries in all of your relationships and how to negotiate (or renegotiate) the terms of some of your most intimate relationships.

Chapter 8 will introduce the patient path to wellness. Healing takes however long it takes, which is okay. This chapter will help you look at how you are approaching this new journey. It will give you some useful tools to use now and to take with you as you move forward.

Chapter 9 will introduce the important practice of taking a step back to gain greater clarity and perspective on your life. Taking a step back emotionally from situations can be useful whenever you are feeling pressured and don't know how to move forward.

Chapter 10 will suggest some possible silver linings in the dark clouds of your parent's depression. It will help you discover what your own silver linings are. When you are able to fully accept with gratitude that you are a child of a depressed parent, your healing will be complete, and your life can begin to unfold in ways you may never have dreamed it would or ever could.

Learning the new skills that you will acquire in this book will help not only you but also your children, if you have any. This book is truly about the hope for and the possibility of intergenerational healing—a healing that transcends space and time. Yes, this path of healing is good for you as an individual—you will be healthier and more joyous because of the skills and practices you will cultivate on this journey—but it can also be a priceless gift and blessing you bestow upon your children and they upon theirs.

This blessing of healing and redemption can stretch forward as far as the eye can see, and your heart can reach. And it begins right here.

CHAPTER 1

When Your Parent Is Depressed

Your past can definitely have an impact on both your present and your future. While it may be too bold to say that your past totally determines your present, it clearly has an impact. What happened then can still matter to you now.

There are specific issues that arise for those of us who grew up with a depressed parent. To understand how this comes about, you need to first take a look back. Imagine you are an archer with a quiver full of arrows. Having found your target, you pull an arrow from your quiver, place that arrow onto the string of your bow, and take your aim. But before you can shoot the arrow, you must first pull the arrow—along with the string—backward, away from your target.

Much of modern therapy has been based upon this principle of going backwards in order to go forward. We go back—examining the past—so we can go forward, stepping boldly into the future.

The past has a powerful hold on our awareness, even if we are healthy and functioning at our best. Sometimes the grip of the past becomes all-consuming, and we cannot seem to move forward in life. This is when the past becomes debilitating. So debilitating that we stand there, stuck, with the arrow drawn back—full of tension and pressure, unable to release it, unable to move forward.

Being unable to move forward, with no confidence that we will hit our target, is one of the main effects of living with depression, whether our own or our parent's. It has probably contributed to your having this book in your hands. Maybe you feel stuck. Maybe you feel frozen and trapped. Whatever your situation is, you can go back and use the past to get a better grip on the present and move forward.

This chapter will help you reflect on your experience of living with a depressed parent. It will help you assess your parent's level of depression and begin to see how your experience as a child has continued to have an impact on you, particularly on your sense of self-worth. The chapter begins with a story that may seem familiar in some ways. We each have our own stories to tell about the past, yet children of the depressed have many experiences in common.

▪ Neil's Story

Neil's dad did all the things that a father is supposed to do. He taught his son how to walk, ride a bike, and drive a car. He wasn't totally absent from Neil's life. Neil knew that his dad cared, even when he was very young and experienced his father becoming enraged at even the littlest things.

Looking back at his dad, Neil can now see the behaviors of a depressed person who had tried to mask the symptoms of that depression with alcohol. As a result of his father's outbursts of anger when he was a child, Neil now has a very hard time with anger, especially his own. In fact, as far as Neil is concerned, anger constitutes such a "hideous display of emotion" that he completely avoids it and anything that might trigger it, including confronting people. Neil is so uncomfortable with feeling anger that he avoids any situation that may result in him becoming like his own father was—angry and enraged, often for no apparent reason.

As a child, Neil can recall wanting to connect and communicate with his dad. He could sense the distress that his dad was experiencing. Like many children of the depressed, Neil wanted to help his father, even if that was not his role and even though he did not know how to actually help him. Neil was sad because he could not have a deeper emotional connection with his father, frustrated because he did not know how to reach his father, and resentful for trying so hard and failing. And yet, he undeniably loved his father. He also felt responsible for who his father was and how he behaved.

As a result, Neil became the communicator that his dad never was. In many ways, it was as if Neil became the parent because his father was missing. If there was a conflict in the family, it was Neil who would seek to resolve it and bring the parties together to communicate with one another.

In later years, Neil realized that his tendencies in relationships were a direct result of how he had wanted to take care of his own father and family as a child. He found it easy to fall into the caretaker role in relationships. But it was impossible to have his own needs met. He was too busy taking care of everybody else's. Neil would then feel the inevitable sadness and frustration he had also felt as a child.

The ghost of his father cast a huge shadow over Neil's life. Even though he no longer lived with his dad, in a very real way his dad still lived within him.

THE MYSTERY OF THE DEPRESSED PARENT

As children, we are quite intuitive. Even when the adults in our lives won't openly discuss an uncomfortable situation like depression in the home, kids know when something isn't quite right—or not at all right. There are many reasons why there may be silence on the topic of depression. Sometimes the absence of discussion results from a simple lack of knowledge and understanding, when the adults themselves don't realize what is going on.

Often the parent who is affected—or the other parent—doesn't want to believe that he or she needs professional help. Following the "If I ignore it, it will get better on its own" strategy, a parent simply may not understand how powerful and effective professional help can be. Alternatively, neither parent may realize that the depressed parent needs help. In other instances, the depressed parent might have sufficient information, and even a diagnosis, but feel too ashamed to talk about things. And sometimes the depression is being treated appropriately, but the adults don't know that it's also important to explain what's going on to the children. No matter what the reason, and whether or not the term "depression" is actually used, children are usually quite aware on some level that depression is present. Mommy or Daddy is not well.

This is when, as children, we attempt to make up our own explanations. If no one is giving us relevant information on which we can base our own understanding, we have no alternative but to grope in the dark for an explanation of what is happening. We say to ourselves, *Mommy is just tired,* or *Daddy just had a bad day at work*, even if Mommy is tired all the time or Daddy has a bad day at work every day.

COMMON CHARACTERISTICS
OF DEPRESSION

Depression can seem to take years from our lives, collapsing long spans of time into a gray sameness where little stands out or registers to us as significant, meaningful, or worthwhile. Just imagine yourself caught in a cloud so all-consuming that you cannot find your way out of it. Imagine an atmosphere so thick and oppressive that you cannot find your bearings. Imagine a state so distraught and debilitating that you cannot even muster the strength to get out of bed in the morning. Now imagine you have children.

To get a better view of the past, it will help to consider what depression is and what depression isn't.

Depression is a mental illness that can be diagnosed, like any other illness, by observing its symptoms (covered in the list that follows) over a period of time. Major depression exists when a cluster of symptoms lasts over a two-week period or more. (What used to be called *dysthymia*, a milder form of depression in which symptoms are experienced over a two-year period or more, is no longer recognized as a separate disorder.) The most recent *Diagnostic and Statistical Manual of Mental Disorders* (DSM; American Psychiatric Association 2013) differentiates depressive disorders not by their severity but rather by the length of time the depression is experienced. Depression may be classified as *chronic*, if it lasts for a long time, or *episodic*, if it lasts for shorter periods. If your parent experienced a long, chronic depression, it would be categorized in the DSM under the umbrella term of "persistent depressive disorder," whether or not your parent's depression was severe or mild.

Depression is not a personality weakness or character flaw. No one chooses to have depression. It is an illness, it can happen to the best and strongest of us, and it should never be judged.

However, even though you probably know this intellectually and rationally, emotionally it can be a different story. For example, you may have felt shame or other bad feelings associated with having a depressed parent. If you've experienced depression yourself, you might have noticed how critical and hard on yourself you can be. To make matters worse, over half of depressed adults are too embarrassed to seek treatment because they regard it as a weakness. Your parent may not have received any treatment for her condition, either because help was unavailable or because it was unsought.

Even if your parent never received a formal diagnosis of depression, there's a good chance that you figured out on your own that he or she was likely depressed, because you witnessed the symptoms of depression. According to the National Institute of Mental Health (2013), here are some of the main symptoms:

- Fatigue and decreased energy

- Loss of interest in once pleasurable interests, activities, or hobbies, including sex

- Feelings of guilt, worthlessness, or helplessness

- Feelings of hopelessness or pessimism

- Persistent sad, anxious, or empty feelings

- Aches or pains, headaches, chest tightness, difficulty breathing, or digestive problems that do not ease, even with treatment

- Insomnia, early-morning wakefulness, or excessive sleeping

- Difficulty concentrating, remembering details, and making decisions

- Overeating or appetite loss

- Thoughts of suicide, and suicide attempts

- Irritability, restlessness

Later this chapter will help you explore whether your parent was mildly, moderately, or severely depressed, but for now it will help to consider more fully what your parent's depression looked like. Here, in a bit more detail, are some characteristics of depression that you might have recognized in your parent:

Pessimism

A depressed person sees the glass half empty instead of half full. Rather than expect a good outcome, the depressed person embraces the downside of any situation. Pessimistic people view the world and situations with negativity, and they expect the worst to happen. Often, they feel hopeless about a difficult situation ever improving.

Feelings of Fatigue

A person experiencing depression usually reports a lack of energy, no matter how much rest or sleep she gets. There is typically little or no motivation to do anything, and the person often feels numb. She experiences little or no enthusiasm and has no interest in activities that once gave pleasure. And a depressed person often doesn't look forward to events that most people would consider fun.

Feeling Overwhelmed

Depression is a thief. It robs you of your joy, your interest in life, and your concern for those you love. Simple tasks feel complicated and difficult, including those that used to be so easy they felt automatic. Normal, daily tasks can suddenly feel like too much. It can also be difficult to make the simplest of decisions.

Short-Temperedness

Depressed people often snap easily and lose their temper quickly. It's typical for a depressed person to regularly and freely lose patience and yell or, at the very least, get angry. It can be scary for children when they never know if the littlest thing might set their parent off.

Having Anxiety

Frequently, anxiety accompanies depression. Your mom or dad may have switched back and forth between nervousness and downward mood swings—or these different moods might have shown up simultaneously. At least half of adults diagnosed with major depression also have an anxiety disorder. You might have noticed that your depressed parent appeared nervous for no apparent reason. Anything (or nothing) could happen in the environment, and this parent would be hand-wringing or biting her nails, furrowing his brow with a worried look, or moving around the house in an agitated manner, unable to be still. If you saw such behaviors, you were witnessing one of the most common symptoms of depression. It's possible that your parent had an anxiety disorder on top of the depression, but depression itself can appear as anxiety.

Feelings of Low Self-Worth

Low self-worth is a symptom of depression. Your depressed parent probably criticized herself and created opportunities to put herself down. He probably felt guilty for absolutely no reason, which added to feelings of low self-worth. Low self-worth reinforces and exacerbates depression.

WHAT CAUSES DEPRESSION

Depression is often quite complex. Though you may want to know why it happened to your parent, it's good to know that you can shed the effects of your parent's depression even if you don't know why it happened. Sometimes there's a clear point we can identify as to the origin of someone's suffering. Sometimes it may be the cumulative impact of certain events, and it can be hard to determine a specific cause. That being said, here are some of the most common causes of depression.

Genetic Roots

Genetics is commonly pointed to as the most frequent cause of depression. A family history of depression clearly does increase your risk, and many researchers hold that depression is passed on through the generations, but exactly how this occurs is unclear. It's important to note that many people with a strong family history of depression will never develop depression themselves. Similarly, people without any family history of depression may become severely depressed at one time or another.

Emotional, Physical, or Sexual Abuse

Abuse of any kind (emotional, physical, or sexual) can eventually lead to depression, even if it occurs years later. A traumatic event, such as a car accident or a life-threatening illness, can also cause depression. Interestingly, it's not the event or situation itself that causes the trauma but the perception of that event or situation by the person who experiences it. In other words, the same event might be traumatic for one person but not another. Personality, temperament, past experiences, and belief systems all play into how people perceive events.

Major Life Events

Short-term depression is often caused by major life events, such as moving, marriage, divorce, isolation, the loss of a loved one, and significant family conflicts. Depression caused by such events usually passes with time and is something most of us feel at one time or another in our lives.

Prolonged Illness and Health Challenges

Certain illnesses and medications can also cause depression. To make matters more confusing, people who are depressed can start self-medicating. Your depressed parent may have started drinking, taking over-the-counter remedies, or abusing prescription drugs to help ease her depressive symptoms. Alcohol is one of the most common drugs used to self-medicate. Ironically, it's a depressant and makes the problem worse.

Other Illnesses with Depression

Chances are you might remember your depressed parent as having certain physical ailments or conditions. Many people with clinical depression also suffer from other illnesses such as diabetes or heart disease. Sometimes it's hard to know which ailment comes first. Serious chronic illness can cause depression, but depression can also weaken the body's immune system in many ways that we're still discovering.

LOOKING AT YOUR OWN SITUATION

Now that you have a better understanding of what depression is, you can better appreciate the state of your parent's mental and emotional inner life when you were a child. Your parent (or both parents) might have been mildly, moderately, or even severely depressed as you were growing up. From your memory, rate the severity of your parent's depression. Typically, the more severe the depression, the harder it is on children of the depressed. But how hard it was on you will also depend on your personality and temperament and on the support systems that were available to you growing up.

Exercise: Rate Your Parent's Level of Depression

On a scale of 1 to 5, in which 1 means not at all, 2 means once in a while, 3 means a few times a week, 4 means frequently, and 5 means all the time, rate how closely these statements describe your parent's experience.

_____ Your parent saw the glass half empty instead of half full, viewed the world and situations with negativity, expected the worst to happen, or was hopeless about situations improving.

_____ Your parent felt tired or lacked energy or needed to sit or lie down during the day.

_____ Your parent expressed little or no enthusiasm, seemed disinterested, or didn't look forward to things.

_____ Your parent was easily overwhelmed, so simple daily tasks felt difficult or impossible to handle.

_____ Your parent was short-tempered, snapped easily, or lacked patience.

_____ Your parent was anxious, nervous for no reason, or worried about anything and everything.

_____ Your parent had low self-worth, felt bad about self, or was often self-critical.

Total your numbers to rate your parent's level of depression:

31 to 35 = severe

26 to 30 = moderate to severe

21 to 25 = moderate

16 to 20 = mild to moderate

11 to 15 = mild

0 to 10 = not symptomatic

Note that this assessment is not meant to offer a psychiatric diagnosis of your parent's depression. Rather, it is to help you think about your experience growing up with your depressed parent and put together the pieces to the puzzle of your upbringing.

Besides recalling such common symptoms as those listed in this assessment, you might recall your parent having other symptoms, such as overeating or experiencing appetite loss, eating either too much or not enough, gaining weight or becoming too thin. Your parent may have had sugar or carbohydrate cravings. Sleep problems are also common with depression. Your depressed parent might have had difficulty sleeping at night or maybe experienced the opposite, sleeping way too much. You may have come home quite often to your parent lying on the couch.

Note: If you witnessed your parent swinging back and forth from way too happy to way too sad and downtrodden, your parent might have had *bipolar disorder*, which involves alternating periods of depression and mania. The complexities of bipolar disorder are beyond the scope of this book, but it's worth mentioning that people with bipolar disorder often show up for help only when they're down. As a result, they can be inappropriately treated for depression alone and given antidepressants, which can cause further problems.

YOUR SENSE OF SELF-WORTH

Growing up with a depressed parent can affect your sense of self-worth as a child and continue to affect your sense of self-worth as an adult.

Exercise: Rate Your Sense of Self-Worth

Place a check mark next to all the statements that you feel are totally true (as opposed to only partially or sometimes true).

_____ *I'm liked for who I really am.*

_____ *I trust my opinions.*

_____ *I enjoy being social.*

_____ *I feel valued.*

_____ *I easily admit when I make a mistake.*

_____ *I deserve to be happy.*

_____ *I deserve respect.*

_____ *I can truly help others.*

_____ *I like myself.*

_____ *When I've done a good job, I can say it.*

_____ *I deserve to be loved.*

_____ *I have important things to say.*

_____ *I accept criticism without feeling ashamed.*

_____ *What others think about me is unimportant, as long as I approve of myself.*

Add up the check marks to get your self-worth score. A score of 11 to 14 checks means that your sense of self-worth is very high, 8 to 10 checks means it is medium, 5 to 7 checks means it is moderate, and less than 5 checks means it is low. Note: If you are feeling bad about a low rating, well, that's just another sign that your sense of self-worth is low.

Keep your self-worth score, and retake the assessment after you have finished this book and implemented some of its advice and ideas. Observe what happens to both your score and your perception of it.

HOPE AND HEALING

The next step is to look at the impact that your parent's depression may have had on you, on your relationship with your parents, on your relationships with your siblings, and on your relationships with significant others later in life. The impact of having had a depressed parent can be far-reaching, continuing to this very day.

As Neil discovered, it may be some time before you realize how your parent's depression has affected you, and you may be only beginning to recognize its impact. But this is also the beginning of your journey toward healing and wholeness. You can take some steps to dramatically improve the quality of your life. Life is short, and depression and its impacts don't need to remain at the forefront of your experience any longer.

KEY POINTS

- Sometimes you need to look back in order to move forward. Evaluating your past and your relationship to your parents can be helpful.

- You may have known something was not quite right with your mother or father, even if you did not know exactly what it was.

- Depression is an illness. It is not something we choose to have happen to us.

- There can be many causes for depression, and determining why your parent was depressed can be difficult. Luckily, you can heal from the impact of your parent's depression even if you don't know why your parent became depressed.

CHAPTER 2

Depression and the Family

Depression is a family matter. A parent's depression affects everyone and every relationship within the family. A depressed parent's fatigue, hopelessness, worrying, and general lack of interest in life and loved ones is disturbing to the family as a whole. Even if your mom or dad got some help and the depression subsided, your family might have continued to experience dysfunction to some degree. Depression—if left untreated—can become the cornerstone upon which every relationship in the family is built.

This chapter outlines some of the ways that having a depressed parent may have affected you and relationships in your family. It offers some exercises to help you process and begin to heal from your own experience growing up with a depressed parent. And it begins with another story that might sound all too familiar.

■ Robyn's Story

As she was growing up, Robyn knew that her mom was depressed. She recalls that when she came home from school in the late afternoon and sat down at the kitchen table to do her homework, her mom would disappear into her bedroom, isolating herself from Robyn and the other children. Robyn didn't know why her mom did that; it was just what she did almost every day. With her mom's habit of shutting herself away from the family, Robyn ended up looking out for her brother and sister, and indeed, Robyn felt as if it were her responsibility to take care of herself and her siblings.

COMMON EFFECTS ON CHILDREN

Many children of depressed parents end up taking on a caretaking role. Because the depressed parent is unavailable—emotionally, mentally, and often physically—children of depressed parents often feel like they have to step up and play the adult role. Clearly, this is not how it *should* be. Ideally, children should be allowed to be children, with the parents doing the parenting. But this structure of relationships is often missing in families in which one of the parents is depressed. In these families, the burden of depression has a way of falling harshly onto the children.

Having a depressed parent is connected with the experience of such problems as social phobia, major depression, behavior disorders, and poorer social functioning in general. About a third of children raised by depressed parents become depressed themselves at some point in their lives. Whether or not your parent also had an anxiety disorder, you could be experiencing anxiety or panic in addition to, or instead of, depression. Generally in families, boys tend to be more affected when their dads are depressed, girls more so when their moms are depressed. Any way you look at it, however, it's clear that parental depression can severely affect children in significant and harmful ways.

Having a depressed parent might mean that you, now, are experiencing depression as an adult. Depression isn't always obvious. If you've been experiencing a mild, low-grade depression as opposed to having severe, debilitating symptoms, it might show itself in subtle ways that you may not have recognized. For instance, you may feel "blah" much of the time, although on the outside you function just fine. Or maybe you don't feel satisfied with your career, social life, or other aspects of your day-to-day. Life may have lost its thrill; or perhaps it never had much thrill to begin with.

With mild depression, it often feels like you're always searching for something else, something different. No matter what you try next, however, you're never completely satisfied. You might be temporarily pleased with the change you've made, but it doesn't last. You may have jumped from job to job, hobby to hobby, and relationship to relationship, always feeling that something's missing.

What Was Missing

If your mom was depressed as you were growing up, she might have been more passive, dependent, and short-tempered and less affectionate with you than your friends' moms were with them; or you might have experienced hostility from her, or sensed tension coming from her direction. If your dad was depressed, he might have been angry and yelled a lot or he might have been very withdrawn. Depression makes it almost impossible to see the brighter side of life, and a parent who's depressed can become very self-involved. Depression is like wearing dark, distorted lenses that filter out anything and everything positive. For a depressed person, life has no color, which makes for a very gray, often quite bleak world.

Depressed parents often complain that their children misbehave. But when children are acting out, it's likely that the chaotic and stressful environment they find themselves in, as well as the poor level of support they receive, is causing or reinforcing their behavioral problems. A depressed parent's negative behavior toward a child can in turn cause behavior issues in the child, which then creates an ongoing, back-and-forth negative pattern. This becomes what the late anthropologist Gregory Bateson (1971) termed a *double-bind*. In it, the child cannot win. Damned if she does, damned if she doesn't.

In addition, a depressed parent often *perceives* children to be difficult and challenging even when the rest of the world doesn't see it that way at all. I remember describing my baby daughter as "fussy" and "high needs." Her dad and grandparents, however, experienced her as happy and easygoing. Postpartum depression distorted my perception; everything in my world felt difficult, including my child. This, in turn, altered my behavior toward my daughter. You can see how easily this kind of back-and-forth cycle can arise.

Having a Depressed Mother

Although there are plenty of exceptions to this generality, depressed moms tend to be less warm and accepting and less tuned in to their children's activities than moms who are not depressed. An extremely depressed mother may even attempt to avoid her child or children. Such avoidance makes sense from the mom's perspective: she can barely take care of herself, let alone another human being who is totally dependent upon her. She may wish desperately that she'd feel normal mom feelings and not have to go through the motions of taking care of her children robotically. She may feel a tremendous amount of guilt, but if she's experiencing major depression, it will not be enough to completely change her behavior.

Children in this circumstance can experience rejection; of course, it's not personal—their parent's illness was never about them—but children will take it personally and perceive it as being about them. If this was your situation, you might have thought, *If I were a better kid, Mom would love me more and give me more attention.* In this way, if your mom was the primary caregiver, you might have developed attachment issues.

How We Are Attached

Attachment theory (Bowlby 1969) describes how the manner in which we relate to others in life is formed in early infancy—especially with our mothers. This theory suggests that how well—or, conversely, how inadequately—you were able to attach to your primary caregiver as an infant forms the basis of your *attachment style*, or way of relating to others.

While there are many intricacies in how we each relate to others, attachment theory generally breaks down these intricacies into two fundamental styles of attachment: *secure* and *insecure*. If your mother, for instance, was depressed, you may never have felt very secure as a child. The message delivered was that relationships are insecure. Or, put another way, relationships equal anxiety. As a result, later in life, you may be insecure about ever having your needs met in virtually any relationship—at least until you come to terms with the effects of being the child of a depressed parent. Only then can you begin taking steps that will allow you to build a better foundation based on a more secure style of attachment.

If you had an insecure attachment to your primary caregiver early in life, the mere prospect of relating to others in any intimate way may give rise to feelings of insecurity and inadequacy. It is easy to understand how relationships in general might be difficult. After all, the first and, some would argue, most important relationship of all was difficult if not impossible. That relationship set the pattern for all subsequent relationships where deep emotional bonds are—or are not—formed.

Depressed Interaction Styles

Depressed parents tend to exhibit certain ways of interacting with their children—or not interacting, as the case may be. Specifically, depressed parents tend to go one of two ways, either neglecting their children or, the opposite, being domineering with them. There is no judgment about your parent's character here. Your parent was doing the best that he or she could at the time, trying to make it from day to day.

NEGLECT

If you were neglected as a child, it doesn't speak to how much your parent loved you. Rather, it is more a matter of how your parent's symptoms were getting in the way of taking care of you. You can assume that your parents did the best that they could. However, like all children, you needed attention and someone who behaved in a caring manner—someone who asked you questions about your day, smiled, and hugged you. What you might have received instead was a gloomy father who sat on the couch watching TV, barely noticing that you were home. If you wanted to go to a friend's house to play, maybe you were rarely asked where, when, how, or with whom—the questions that convey *I care about you* to a child.

Children raised by a depressed parent often feel like they must be responsible for themselves, since the adult in their life isn't monitoring them. Such children can feel like they are raising themselves. Sometimes these children turn out to be ultraresponsible as adults but not very good at having fun, since they felt that they had to be their own parent growing up.

Often it feels to the child as if the neglect must be your fault—as if you aren't worth the attention—or your parent's depression and inability to care for you is somehow your fault. Children are notorious for taking responsibility for what's happening in the home, even for circumstances clearly beyond their control, such as the moods and behaviors of one or both parents.

INVASIVENESS

Another common (although less frequent) interaction style that depressed parents can use with their children is being overly involved in their lives, sometimes to the point of being domineering. This feels invasive to the child, since the parent is continuously asking unnecessary questions about the child's whereabouts (including within the house), activities, and choices. If this was your situation, you may have felt stifled. You may have often experienced a desire to push your parent away but been afraid of the consequences—your parent's anger or hurt—which might have left you with a sense of guilt and a feeling of responsibility.

A depressed parent can swing from one style to the other and back again, so a kind of back-and-forth phenomenon between styles can occur. In this case, you might think, *Sometimes Mom was withdrawn and ignored me, and other times she was in my face and would drive me crazy.* It may be that you never knew what to expect.

EFFECTS ON SIBLING RELATIONSHIPS

Depressed parents often play favorites, treating one or more of their children better than others, which can make less favored children resent a sibling's very existence. This inconsistent treatment can have a negative effect on the quality of sibling relationships: brothers and sisters will typically argue and fight and be unsupportive of each other.

Children of depressed parents may have more behavioral issues than average, either internalizing their troubles by withdrawing or experiencing anxiety or depression, or externalizing them with temper tantrums, aggressive behavior, or rule breaking. When siblings have relationships based on conflict and competition, they typically develop problems with their peers.

On the other side of this, strong sibling relationships can act as a buffer against the effects of parental depression. Close sibling relationships can protect children from some of the negativity associated with having a depressed parent or parents. As Neil from chapter 1 explained, "My sister always understood my dad, since she had a tendency toward depression, too. I honestly don't know what I would have done without my sister. We took care of each other in a mutually beneficial way. We would always support each other. If my dad was being weird and my mom didn't want to talk about it, I could just go hang out with my sister. If she hadn't been there, I imagine I would have left the house more often, just to get away from everything."

It's also good to know that if your other parent, the one who wasn't depressed, was warm, attentive, and close with you and your siblings, it may have helped to prevent some of the worst effects of having a depressed parent.

The next exercise will help you look at your relationship with your sibling or siblings as you were growing up.

Exercise: Remember Your Sibling Relationship

Think about your relationship with your brother or sister. If you had more than one sibling, choose the brother or sister with whom you were closest. Now complete these next two sentences with the statement that fits your situation the best:

When your parents argued or fought, you

- hung out with your sibling (spent more time with your brother or sister when your parents weren't getting along or when your depressed parent was detached, withdrawn, angry, or emotionally absent)

- didn't spend more time with your sibling (stayed in your room when there was friction or tension between your parents, put on headphones to drown out the noise, isolated yourself, or left the house)

When you were growing up, you

- were grateful to have a brother or sister to be with (looking back, you feel thankful for having the brother or sister that you had)

- didn't like having a sibling (felt in competition with your sibling or felt that one or both of your parents were treating your brother or sister better than you)

- didn't care one way or the other that you had a sibling (it wasn't a help or a hindrance, since you each handled uncomfortable situations in the home in your own way)

If you had a difficult relationship with your sister or brother as you were growing up, you may very well continue to have difficulties in your relationship today.

Again, having a depressed parent can complicate sibling relationships. As an adult, you may feel closer to your sibling because of the difficulties you shared, or you may be farther apart.

If You Were an Only Child

Being an only child of a depressed parent has its own difficulties. There was no buffer. There was no other sibling to help take the weight off, relieve the pressure, or absorb the frustration and shame. You may have felt isolated. If you are the only child of a depressed parent, you may still be ashamed of your mother or father and to this day be unwilling to share the harsh reality of your past, even with your closest friends.

Jennifer's experience as a child is especially telling, in this regard: "I didn't have any siblings, and I think it was a curse. There wasn't anybody to share anything with. My fantasy was that if there had been somebody else in the family, at least I would have had somebody else to talk to. I couldn't talk to anybody about my situation, not my closest friends, nobody. No one knew my mother was an alcoholic and depressed."

What a heavy burden to have to shoulder all alone. But if you were an only child, you can help yourself heal and move on from your painful memories. Similarly, if you had difficulties with your siblings, this is something you can work on and heal.

Whatever your experience was, what's important to remember is that it's not just the past that affects you but also your memory and perception of the past. The next exercise will help you take a trip back to imagine events differently. Obviously this doesn't and cannot change what actually occurred, but redoing past events in your mind can soften your feelings about the past by altering what's been encoded in your psyche.

Exercise: Adult Time Travel

Find a comfortable place to sit or lie down, where you won't be disturbed. Complete each of these next steps, taking as much time as you need for each one.

1. Imagine a scenario when you were young and when your depressed parent withdrew or got angry or behaved in some other way that upset you.

2. Label how you felt, using words such as "hurt," "sad," "angry," "worried," "betrayed," abandoned," "guilty," or "responsible." Use whatever words pop into your head. This step can be challenging if you're not familiar with labeling your feelings (and as a child, you may have just felt "icky"), but it's good for you to practice putting descriptive words to feelings.

3. Continue to envision this scenario while adding yourself into the picture as the adult you are now, traveling back in time to visit your younger self so that you're standing right next to him or her. Your job is to give your younger self whatever you needed but didn't receive at that time. Think about what that might have looked or sounded like—there's no right or wrong answer here, and there are no rules (except that violence isn't allowed during this exercise toward people or things, even in your imagination). If you had a sibling, but you weren't close, you might imagine that you were close. Alternatively, if you didn't have a brother or sister, you could create one in your mind. What would your sibling have said to you during this tough time?

4. Imagine putting your arm around your younger self and saying whatever you needed to hear back then. For instance, "This is really hard right now, but you'll be okay. None of this is your fault. I'm here to protect you and take care of you. Do you want to go to the movies or play ball outside?"

5. If you are feeling emotional, you can cry. Strong responses are healthy and welcome. If you don't feel anything welling up inside, that's okay too. If you're feeling angry and resisting the exercise thinking this is the corniest thing in the world, that's good to know too. The truth is you may need this exercise more than ever. After you calm down a bit, try it again from the beginning and see if it's a little easier. Be aware of any sensations, including any physical ones.

6. Once the younger you feels totally filled up and satisfied with the time traveler's comfort and support, reassure your younger self that you'll be there anytime he or she needs you in the future. If it feels right to give this little person a hug, do it, and with a smile, say goodbye for now.

Allow yourself to sit with your feelings as you come out of this exercise. You may notice that you feel calmer. Perhaps you feel a little lighter, as you experience some relief from the heavy burden of difficult memories.

If you found this exercise helpful, you can use it often, especially when an uncomfortable memory or feeling comes up that's associated with your past. It's important to learn how to be there for yourself, to give yourself what you may have needed but not have received as a child. Later chapters will give you more exercises to help you do this.

YOUR PARENTS' RELATIONSHIP

The quality of your parents' relationship directly affected you, for better or for worse. Whether your parents were married or divorced, they had a relationship of some kind with each other. If you were raised by a single parent, maybe your parent had a significant other. What matters is how the adults in your life behaved with each other as you were growing up, for that relationship sent an explicit message to you about how relationships work or, alternatively, don't work.

Many children of the depressed are also children of divorced parents. Depression in a partner is one of the best predictors of difficulties in marriages. When those difficulties lead to divorce, however, it's not the depression in and of itself that's the culprit. Rather, it's the lack of proper help for the people involved that can eventually cause couples to break up.

When one spouse is depressed, the other spouse often feels resentment or anger. For instance, your mom might have been outgoing and fun-loving before her depression. If so, once her depression hit, your dad probably felt frustrated and upset with her—especially if he wasn't receiving adequate emotional support. Your father might have wondered why your mother didn't just "lighten up." He may have wondered why she had "changed." He may have even expressed to her—or to you or your siblings—something along the lines of "I just wish we had your old mom back with us."

In an ideal world, we would all be supportive of one another. Regardless of what challenges or issues came our way, we would offer support, comfort, and encouragement to those we love. This, though, is not always the case. In the real world, changes like depression are often met with a partner's anxiety, concern, worry, anger, and frustration: "How come you can't just be like you used to be? We used to have so much fun and we enjoyed life. What happened?" Unfortunately, depression simply does not go away by wishing it away.

When a spouse's depression lingers, the partner's frustration can grow and mount, which can in turn exacerbate the depressed person's condition and have an impact on everyone in the family. In the best of circumstances, the nondepressed spouse understands what is taking place, which helps everyone, particularly the children in the family.

Exercise: Remembering Your Parents' Relationship

Take a moment to remember what the atmosphere was like in your home when you were young. Think about how your nondepressed parent reacted to your depressed parent. Now rate how closely each statement matches your own experience. Use a scale of 1 to

5, where 1 means that your parent hardly responded this way at all and 5 means your parent almost always responded this way. If a particular response does not at all describe your parent's behavior, don't assign any number to it. Note: If both of your parents were depressed, you can complete this exercise for one parent and then for the other, since each may have responded differently.

_____ Your nondepressed parent was loving and compassionate toward your depressed parent. For example, you heard: "Let's get you some help." "I'm sorry you're suffering." "We'll get through this together. I'm here for you." "This isn't your fault."

_____ Your nondepressed parent grew frustrated and impatient. For example, you heard: "Just stop it!" "I'm tired of this!" "Can't you just be happy?" "When are you going to be normal?"

_____ Your nondepressed parent ignored the depressed parent, acting as if the depressed parent were invisible, or seemed to have no reaction at all.

_____ Your nondepressed parent seemed to be going through the motions, had a flat affect, or had no emotional response at all, but at least physically took care of the depressed spouse.

_____ Your nondepressed parent was worried and anxious. This parent might or might not have been compassionate but mostly expressed concern about the present and the future.

_____ Your nondepressed parent became depressed too.

If your nondepressed parent was mostly loving and compassionate, then you and your siblings greatly benefited. In contrast, if your nondepressed parent was often or almost always frustrated and impatient, you most likely were affected by the negativity between your parents. Likewise, if your nondepressed parent ignored your depressed parent, just went through the motions, or was often worried and anxious around your depressed parent, this would have had a negative impact on you. If you experienced your nondepressed parent getting sucked into the depression, that would be especially difficult, since, at least temporarily, you would have lost this parent too.

What set the atmosphere in your home growing up was in large part your parents' relationship. Given that at least one of your parents was depressed, how your other parent responded to him or her would be critical to that atmosphere. The more unresolved tension and hostility between your parents, the greater the possibility that you would be affected. But remember, no matter how high the level of stress was between your parents, you can and will emerge healthy with the steps you're now taking.

Depression Can Be Contagious

In a worst-case scenario, the stress of taking care of a partner who is depressed can trigger depression in the caretaker. If your dad was depressed and your mom was the caretaker, for example, she may have become depressed as a result, especially if she didn't receive adequate attention or support. Then you, the child growing up in such a family, would have two depressed parents to contend with.

Living with a depressed partner places a huge burden on the other partner. Being the caregiver of a depressed partner limits outside relationships, and family problems may interfere with job and career. Besides taking care of their depressed partner, caregivers usually must finish tasks that the depressed spouse lacks the energy to complete. If the caretaker has to take time off from work because of increased responsibilities at home, the family income may drop, which can contribute to the cycle of increasing stress and higher levels of depression. This adds to the strain on the marriage, which makes everything worse for everyone in the family.

Good support, provided by other adult family members or outside help, can make a huge difference for the nondepressed spouse and the family. Without support, partners can begin having ugly interactions, which make everyone feel worse. Name-calling, put-downs, criticisms, and other hurtful actions between partners can damage the relationship and the children. Even if children only witness the unpleasantness, they are harmed by it. For solid mental health and social adjustment, kids need to feel secure about their parents' relationship. When parents have conflicts that are unresolved, the kids can become depressed or anxious, and have other behavioral problems as well. Constant arguing between parents without any problem solving affects the child's trust in others. Having parents who insult each other and who are hostile toward each other in any way can greatly damage a child's well-being.

You may want to take a moment now to consider the health of your significant relationships today, whether you are married, living with someone, or in a seriously committed relationship. Later, this book will examine specific issues that may arise in intimate relationships, for children of the depressed often struggle in their adult relationships because of the unique challenges that arise from having a depressed parent.

LOOKING FORWARD

The purpose of this chapter was to give you a better sense of how having a depressed parent influenced all the members in your family. It helped you explore your sibling relationships and your parents' relationship and asked you to consider how possible problems between your parents might have affected you, then and now. Acknowledging your emotions (even if you couldn't label them as you were growing up), discovering how to get more support in your life, and developing your self-worth and value are some of the next steps you will take on this journey.

KEY POINTS

- Depression affects the whole family.

- How parents relate to their children is affected in dramatic ways by the presence of depression.

- Healing and treatment is not just about (or for) the depressed parent.

- Parental depression can have an impact on sibling relationships, causing competition or, alternatively, reinforcing solidarity.

- An only child of depressed parents can suffer feelings of extreme isolation.

- Depression can impact marriages negatively and can be contagious, resulting in either divorce or a second depressed parent.

CHAPTER 3

Opening the Door to a Happier, Healthier You

It takes a great deal of courage to want to get better, to want to heal. It may be hard to admit that you have a problem. You may be just starting to realize that you were the child of a depressed parent or resisting the idea that your parent was, in fact, depressed. You may find the past hard to face in part because of the stigma surrounding the issue of mental health. You may feel shame or other difficult feelings associated with having a depressed parent. It also may take a while for the full implications of your situation to set in. Even if you are aware of what happened to you as a child and how having a depressed parent has affected you, you may have a difficult time imagining your life could change for the better. This chapter will cover these obstacles and help you address them, opening the door to a happier, healthier you.

HOW TO ACKNOWLEDGE
THE PAST

Many people struggle with the devastating aftereffects of depression in the family while being unaware of the trauma they experienced as children. When they are finally able to look back upon their past, they often suddenly realize that while they knew something was a bit different about their early years, they had no idea that their mother or father was depressed for much of their childhood.

If you are in your forties or fifties, there was less general awareness of depression and mental illness when you were a child than there is today; you may be only now coming to terms with the implications of your childhood—what it meant for you, how it formed you, how it still impacts your life experience.

You may have trouble acknowledging that your parent was depressed and that this has had an impact on your own mental health whatever your age. You may feel uncomfortable admitting that you have mental health challenges. Think of it this way: You wouldn't avoid admitting it if you had a debilitating physical health condition. It's important to treat your mental health with as much respect as you would treat your physical health. Likewise, you may feel uncomfortable labeling your parent as a depressed person. But the road to better health is not about demonizing your parents. It is not about scapegoating, or using the past as an excuse to explain why your present is the way it is.

Delving into the past is important, precisely because there is still such a deep cultural stigma regarding mental illness. It is important because there is still so much shame around mental health challenges like depression. It is important because, even to this day, far too many people suffer in silence, ashamed and afraid to open up about their own experience. It is important because to get better, we first must admit to ourselves that our parents were depressed, and that to some degree the effects of that depression still linger on to this day. Only then can we begin to heal.

Emotional Obstacles

Imagine the difference between telling someone that you grew up with a mother who struggled with breast cancer and telling someone that you grew up with a mother who struggled with depression. For most of us, the first task might bring up some difficult memories, but we would have no problem describing what went on, how it impacted us (to the degree we were aware of it), and how our present adult life takes into account what happened when we were children. But if we are attempting to tell someone about how we grew up with a depressed parent, all sorts of obstacles can get in the way, including shame, rationalizations, guilt, denial, and fear. Consider whether any of these obstacles are in your way.

SHAME

I had good solid friendships growing up, but I wasn't allowed to have friends come into our house. I don't remember my parents even once having their friends over for dinner. If someone was coming to pick me up, I would wait outside. If they came to the door, I wouldn't let them in. I always felt very ashamed of this.

Shame doesn't let anyone in. Not even friends. Maybe especially not even friends.

What would others think of me if they found out what my life was like and how I really lived? What would they think of me if they discovered that one of my parents was depressed? Almost certainly, if they knew about my situation, I would not have had any friends at all. After all, if my parents were struggling with a mental illness, then it would have only stood to reason that others would assume that I might be "crazy" too.

This is why shame makes it so hard for people to get help. It won't allow you to let anyone in to see what is really going on. The true nature of your experience is kept out of sight.

Getting help is the first step, and even your purchase of this book may have required a monumental effort of will and determination. After all, when you were at the bookstore, you held this book with its title clearly showing in your hand as you proceeded to the checkout stand. Maybe it was a local bookstore where you might run into someone you know. Maybe you even know the cashier personally. What would the cashier think of you then? What would everyone think when it eventually got around. Maybe they would talk: "Did you hear about so-and-so and the book they bought the other day? I wonder if it is going to happen to her, too, someday. Maybe it already has!"

These are not crazy thoughts. When you grow up in a home with a depressed parent, there is often a great deal of shame that comes along with it. That shame is, in my experience, one of the biggest obstacles to overcome on the path of healing. We are afraid of what others would think of us if they only knew the truth.

It is shame that keeps many trapped in silence for far too long. Years of unnecessary suffering can add up, one on top of the other. True joy is never discovered, let alone lived. Joy is for other people, anyway. People who did not grow up with depressed parents.

RATIONALIZATIONS

It's not that bad. It actually could have been a lot worse. I am sure there are people whose parents had bigger problems than mine when I was growing up. Sure, my dad was depressed a lot of the time, and it really affected our relationship when I was a kid. But I have learned to deal with it.

Rationalizations can sound a lot like positive thinking. And who doesn't want to be positive? I am sure we have all tried our best, at some point, to muster up the strength to frame some of our toughest challenges in a positive light. It's good to look at the bright side, right?

Not all the time. The problem with rationalizations is that they can keep us from honestly assessing our circumstances, making any necessary adjustments, and then moving forward. Rationalizations are the fool's gold of positive thinking. They seem valuable—like real personal growth—but they are worthless, for they keep us stuck in the same situation and circumstances, doing the same thing, living the same lives and lies, over and over again.

Rationalizations can often sound like acceptance. It may seem as if we have really come to understand the nature of our upbringing, in terms of the impact that our parent's depression had upon us, and then experienced a dramatic shift in which we have fully accepted and embraced what this meant for us, both then and now. However, rationalizing is not the same as deeply accepting and healing ourselves. It keeps us from truly exploring our past and present situations, grasping how depression has affected us, and working to move on. Ultimately, rationalizing is not only a long way from a healed and healthy state but an actual impediment to achieving that state of being.

GUILT

What if I did something that made my parent depressed? What if it was all my fault? Maybe if I had never been born, my mom would have been okay. What if it was my being around that made her depressed?

Guilt can be a particularly cruel obstacle, one that blots out the light of our potential healing. When we take responsibility for our parent's depression, when we blame ourselves, when we feel guilty for existing and seemingly causing so much distress, there is no hope for our own healing. Guilt locks the door to the path of our healing. As long as we listen to the voice of guilt, a large part of us will remain imprisoned behind that door.

DENIAL

My parent had bad days. Sure. I bet everyone's mom or dad had a bad day now and then.

When you deny there is a problem, the possibility of things being different never enters the picture. Perhaps you can sense how denial not only invites a certain degree of stasis—by refusing to entertain the possibility that something could be tragically wrong—but can also invite us into a downward spiral. It is not hard to see that an unaddressed issue will tend to fester and grow.

Luckily, you probably haven't experienced this stage, or if you did experience it, you have moved out of it. If you were still stuck under the spell of denial, it's unlikely that you would be reading this book.

FEAR

What if my unfortunate upbringing is true? What if I cannot deny it any longer? What if I cannot rationalize my way out of how I feel up to this very day? What if I'm doomed for a lifetime of depression too? And what does it mean if my guilt is undeniably real?

The common denominator of shame, guilt, rationalizations, and denial is fear. The problem with these states is that the fear they inspire keeps us from moving forward, from healing our past. Just as someone who is truly scared is said to be "frozen in place," fear can paralyze us. When it's really powerful, fear can prevent us from opening the door to our own healing. In other words, it can keep us from the happier, healthier, and more fulfilled version of ourselves that beckons us forward.

How You May Be Feeling

Beginning on the journey to overcome the challenges you have faced in the past may occasionally leave you feeling unsteady. You may feel awkward, anxious, unsure, timid, shy, and even stubborn. Changing the way we are can be difficult. You have probably lived a certain way for as long as you can remember. Even if it comes with a degree of suffering that has made you all too ready for change, the way you've been may nevertheless have been all you've known for a very long time.

This means that even if you have opened the door to your own healing, you may still feel like there are a lot of compelling reasons to go back through that door and close it again. The voices of denial and shame, guilt and rationalizations, can still have a powerful draw. When we are feeling anxious and afraid about openly sharing our experiences and memories, it's easy to fall into old patterns. We know these negative voices. They have been with us, virtually, our entire life. *Maybe they are right,* you may think. *It really isn't that bad. I'll be okay. Things will all work out just fine.* It is that kind of rationalizing that, while seemingly positive, can prevent you from taking positive steps.

Exercise: Hearing Your Negative Voices

Take a few moments now to write down your own negative voices. Some of what you've been telling yourself is probably so familiar that the lines can roll out all too easily. Write them all down in a list titled "Lies I Tell Myself" or "My Negative Voices," so that you're clear that these are the damaging beliefs that you need to question. You can use the space provided or write in your journal.

Once you've purged your mind of these thoughts as much as you're able, examine your list. Are the voices full of shame? Rationalizations? Guilt? Denial?

Just remember: at the bottom of all this thinking lies fear, and while your fear seems to be protecting you, it may be preventing you from becoming the person you have truly always been and want to become again. Acknowledging that fear is how you begin to overcome it.

FINDING THE SUPPORT YOU NEED

Two things we all need the most on our healing journey are probably the very things that were in shortest supply as we were growing up: support and encouragement.

"It'll be okay. You can do this. I am here for you." These are the kinds of sentiments not often voiced or heard in a home where a depressed parent lives. In fact, it may be just the opposite. You heard: "Things are not going to be okay. I don't know what to do. And it's all up to me." Because your mother or father was debilitated by depression, there may have been times when there was no emotional support and encouragement available for you. Your resources in that department may have been virtually nonexistent. If you didn't develop them then, you need to develop them now.

Sometimes depressed parents offer the support and encouragement we need but are unable to offer themselves similar support and encouragement. If this happened in your family, you may have had such thoughts as these: *If Mom doesn't feel good about herself, why should I? If Dad calls himself stupid, maybe I am too.* This illustrates how it's never enough for parents to offer support just to their children. They also need to offer it to themselves, so they're modeling this healthy mentality to their kids. Once depressed parents receive help and can offer themselves the same support and encouragement they offer their children, it automatically helps their children.

As a child of a depressed parent, you faced significant challenges that others did not face. While other children were being supported and encouraged, you may have been wondering what was wrong with your mother or father and if and when they were ever going to be okay. As discussed in chapter 2, when this becomes the norm in families, children become insecure. This insecurity lasts into adulthood, not only in the belief that *No one will ever really be there for me in the ways that I need,* but also in the sense of feeling incapable of meeting the challenges that arise in the normal course of living. Examples of this might include looking for a new job, taking care of a newborn child, managing your aging parent's decline into dementia, or handling some sort of health crisis of your own. Not having been given the kind of support and encouragement you needed as a child can leave a lasting impression in this way: normal challenges can feel overwhelming; really significant ones can feel utterly impossible.

DEVELOPING YOUR SELF-WORTH AND VALUE

It goes without saying that every child deserves unconditional love. Many children receive such unconditional love, but many others do not. If your mother or father was depressed when you were a child, then your worth and value may not have been made clear to you. In fact, you may never have received the positive messages that you needed. Your parent probably felt overwhelmed by the everyday tasks of being a parent. Such struggles no doubt affected you and left a dramatic impact. Even if your parent loved you dearly, given the very nature of depression, he or she may not have been able to express this love to you in a consistent way. The result was that your sense of worth and value may have been unclear to you. In other words, without your mother or father's support and encouragement, you may have never experienced or realized your unique worth and value as a child. This issue may linger today, but you can do something about it. You can give yourself the support and encouragement that you never received as a child. You can tell yourself a new story.

As children, we don't have the option of telling ourselves a different story. If our parents do not consistently convey our worth and value to us, then we may end up assuming that we don't have much inherent value. If our parents had issues with anger and depression and felt overwhelmed both by life in general and by the role of being a parent, then chances are we were probably given the message that our unique value and worth as human beings was, at best, minimal and, at worst, missing altogether.

You even may have received the message that you were a burden to your mother or father. More than one client, over the years, has shared that they ended up feeling like their mother or father wished they had never been born. It is hard to imagine a blow more deadly to your sense of worth, value, and self-esteem.

Cultivating Support and Encouragement

As you begin this journey of healing, you will need to find in others around you or in yourself the support and encouragement that was lacking in your childhood. Even the simplest words of support will help make you once again feel and claim a sense of self-worth and value. Often knowing that someone cares is enough. It can give you the encouragement you may need to make it through a rough day.

Men and women alike, of all ages and ethnicities, have come to me feeling overwhelmed by the simple tasks of daily life. By offering support and encouragement, I do my best to make sure that they know two extremely important things. The first is that they are worthy and valuable people, and the second is that they are capable of skillfully handling whatever it is that life has in store for them. You too need to know that you are a worthy and valuable person, and that you are capable of skillfully handling whatever life has in store.

The support and encouragement you need is neither mysterious nor highly technical. Many of us can believe that the problems we face are far too complex to understand or solve. But with support and encouragement, we can begin to take simple steps to deal with our problems, steps that are neither mysterious nor monumental and have been proven to be highly effective over time.

One simple strategy for developing self-worth and value is to offer someone else a word of support or encouragement when you can see that they are having a bad day. Doing this is as simple as saying, "I believe in you. I know that whatever is going on right now, you are capable of handling it with grace and dignity. And if you stumble, that's okay, too. Stumbling simply means that you're cultivating new skills. I'll be there to help you get back up if you need me."

While it may seem that offering others support and encouragement has little to do with feeling supported and encouraged, it actually has everything to do with it. You may ask yourself, *How can I give what I don't have?* But the mere act of offering someone a simple gesture of support and encouragement tells you that you have support and encouragement within yourself to give. And offering others support and encouragement also can serve to get you out of yourself. It's the very opposite of emphasizing your own plight by fixating on what you are missing.

Practice drinking in self-support as you hand it to others, and you'll feel its positive boost. As you say to a colleague, "Good for you. That took guts, and you did it," allow your words to filter right into your own heart as a gift from yourself to yourself.

GRIEVING THE MOTHER OR FATHER YOU NEVER HAD

Before you can move further on this healing journey, you need to consciously grieve for that child that you were—the child who may not have received what was needed. It is almost as if our grief were a weight that holds us back and wears us down. If we can find ways to move through our grief over not having the parent (or parents) we deserved—that we wanted, that we wished we could have had—then we can release the weight of that grief. We can move forward.

It's not enough to act strong, put on a brave face, and pretend like everything is okay when it may not be. You may have done this at times in the past. You may even be doing this right now. You may be afraid to feel what you honestly feel about your mother or father having been depressed. It may scare you. Maybe you'd rather not go there.

However, it is vital to process our grief, for unprocessed grief inevitably comes out in dysfunctional ways that do great harm to us and to others. It is often this grief that is behind drug and alcohol addictions. It is grief—the emotions we don't want to feel, the memories we don't want to remember—that is behind such attempts to escape and numb our pain. The last thing we really want to do is to feel it all, and yet this is what we must do. We simply cannot heal if we avoid our pain. It is, paradoxically, in facing our pain that we can create the hope of healing.

Let me be clear here: I am not advocating that you drown in your own sorrow or suffering. That is not what this is about. Besides, that would be no better than drowning in alcohol. But if you do not honestly acknowledge and engage the sorrow you have over not being met and honored by your depressed parent, then you are only exacerbating the problem, not addressing it. It was your mother or father's inability to meet you fully that left you with a wound that you are now attempting to heal. Avoiding or ignoring that wound—to not embrace that hurt child that still lives inside of you—would serve only to reenact what caused the damage in the first place.

Moving Past Your Grief

There is a general principle in psychology that what we don't embrace we can't replace. Another way of stating this is that "what we resist persists." Avoiding our grief is a surefire way to make sure that it lingers. Again, giving our grief a voice is vital. Feeling sorrow is okay. In fact, it is more than okay. It is, in large part, what makes us human. What I promise is that you won't need to stay in the place of grief for long. It will be temporary. As it's removed, you'll have space for what you really want: joy, enthusiasm, passion, and purpose.

Thirteenth-century Persian poet Rumi believed that we did not have to find love. He believed that we are made of love and made for love. All we have to do is remove that which is in love's way. If we can get rid of the obstacles blocking out love's light, then what is left?

As children, we come into the world primed for love—we are innocent and pure. We are also very vulnerable, because we exist in a state that is utterly dependent upon others. This means that how we are, or are not, treated can have a tremendous impact upon us. Through no fault of our own, the light of love in our own hearts can be blocked out. If the love in our hearts is blocked, it can affect us greatly, which is why it is so important to consciously acknowledge this problem and work through it.

HOW TO SUPPORT YOURSELF

When struggling with the chorus of shame, guilt, denial, and rationalizing all singing their dark and damning songs, you will need to find support and encouragement. Here are some strategies you can use to support and encourage yourself on this challenging journey.

- Watch a feel-good movie. Pick out a movie that is inspiring or has an uplifting message.

- Read the biography or autobiography of someone who triumphed over insurmountable odds.

- Be gentle with yourself. Take your time. Relax. You deserve your own kindness.

- Eat well. Get enough rest. Breathe.

- Take a good walk. Never underestimate the beneficial impact of walking, especially in nature.

- Call an old friend and reconnect. Reach out to someone with whom you have lost touch.

- Listen to some soothing music. Classical music, especially, seems to synchronize brain waves and induce a relaxation response.

- Volunteer your time working with those less fortunate than yourself. It is amazing how much we can feel supported by offering some support to others who also need it.

- Spend time investing in a hobby or recreational activity that you enjoy. It could be anything from bird-watching to building model planes, from quilting to learning how to play the piano.

- Again…breathe!

- Laugh. Be silly. Be playful. Remember, you do not need to be serious all the time.

- Watch children play. It can be your own children. It can be your grandchildren. It can be children at the park. Notice how much exuberance they have for life. It can be infectious.

These are some ideas to get you started. You should feel free to use what has already given you support in your own life and to call on those who have offered you encouragement in the past. In other words, find a way to make this list your own by trying out different things and adding to it based on what has worked for you both now and in your past.

THE NEXT STEP

The opening chapters of this book have introduced how a parent's depression can come to affect us as children. The next chapter will help you look more closely at how this happens in the realm of our thoughts and thinking habits and how you can change these thoughts and thinking habits to improve your life.

KEY POINTS

- This journey of healing requires courage.

- Feeling guilt, shame, fear, and denial and trying to rationalize away issues is common at the outset.

- Grief is real. It needs to be embraced, and you need to allow yourself to grieve properly for what you didn't receive as a child so that your sorrow can be replaced with joy, enthusiasm, passion, and purpose.

- It's important to find ways to support and encourage yourself on your journey, and to connect with and surround yourself with supportive and encouraging people.

CHAPTER 4

Thinking Better About Yourself

No two people or their experiences are ever completely the same. Everyone's different, yet among the children of depressed parents, certain themes do seem to apply regardless of personality or specific circumstances. We each have our own story to tell, and yet our stories have much in common. This chapter will explore how children of the depressed often share certain learned thinking patterns and habits, forming stories that we tell ourselves about our lives; and it will explore how these stories may be serving us poorly. More specifically, it will help you look at your own thoughts and narratives and learn how to replace less helpful thoughts and narratives with more supportive ones about yourself and your life.

■ Jennifer's Story

Growing up as an only child, there was a lot of pressure on Jennifer. It seemed to Jennifer that her mother projected all of her own dreams and desires onto her child and demanded that Jennifer succeed—at any cost. Jennifer can recall practicing the piano with her mother by her side. When Jennifer made a mistake, her mother responded by whacking her on the hands so viciously that she would run outside to seek her father's protection. Sadly for Jennifer, her father seemed to be afraid, too, and refused to intervene on her behalf.

Looking back, Jennifer can see how her mother's rage and alcoholism—stemming from her undiagnosed and untreated depression—not only kept Jennifer in line but also did the same to her father. Neither of them dared cross her mother—lest she be provoked to fits of rage and abuse. Father and daughter both walked on eggshells and did everything they could to avoid upsetting "Momma."

For Jennifer, the ultimate trial of her childhood was that she could not talk to anyone about what life was like for her. Certainly, she could not speak with her mother about it. Her father was in denial and didn't want to rock the boat. He seemed to believe that everything would be okay if they could just avoid discussing it. He could not—or would not—even protect his own daughter. With no one to share her story with, Jennifer was alone.

THE BURDEN OF UNTOLD TALES

Being unable to tell our story and share our actual experience—for whatever reason—can be damaging to our well-being. It can be challenging enough to have to deal with whatever struggles happen to befall us. It is far more challenging if we feel we can't share what is going on within us. Untold stories can result in depression, as the weight of our untold tales depletes us and wears us down over time. It can lead to addiction, in one form or another, as we try to distract or numb ourselves.

As you begin to be honest with yourself and others about what happened, you can start to ask yourself some important questions: Is the story you are telling yourself about your life helping you, or is the story hurting you? What kinds of thoughts accompany the story you tell yourself? Are they helpful thoughts, or are they harmful or hurtful thoughts?

The stories that we tell ourselves can have an impact on our experience of life. Depending on the stories, they can make life harder or more enjoyable.

Are the thoughts and feelings that come from—and are a part of—the story that you tell yourself about your life supportive and encouraging? Do you feel empowered by the thoughts and feelings that accompany the story that you tell yourself, or do you feel defeated by those thoughts and feelings? For example, do you tell yourself things like, *It will never get better. This is how I am. It will always be like this. I am doomed because of my childhood*, and so on?

Listening to Your Own Story

It's important to listen closely to what your inner storyteller is saying. We each have a voice inside our head, and this inner storytelling voice interprets what things mean, what we think of ourselves, and what our hopes and ambitions are. It also narrates our fears and failings. Take a moment right now to get acquainted with your own inner storyteller. Stop reading for a minute, so you can listen to your inner storyteller's voice. Then continue reading.

What is the story that you hear? Maybe your inner storyteller is telling you a story about how silly it is to stop and introduce yourself to him. Maybe your story goes something like this:

This is all nonsense. How is this going to help me? An inner storyteller? This is absurd! I can't believe I am wasting my time like this. I am definitely not introducing myself to my inner storyteller. I don't even have one. It's all just me. This is nonsense.

Your inner storyteller's criticism, telling you that this is all nonsense, is in itself a story. The fact is that we are constantly telling ourselves what things mean, and, it's all made up. That is the function of stories. Assigning a meaning and judging the things that happen to us is telling a story.

It's important to listen to the stories that your inner story-teller tells you. Only then can you begin to ask yourself questions about the stories you hear. Later, you will learn some specific practices that will help you see that your inner storyteller is at best like that friend who will never stop talking and at worst your own worst enemy. For now, be willing to accept the notion that not everything that comes from your inner storyteller is the gospel truth.

Interpreting Your Story

No one can change what happened in the past. No matter how empowered we become as individuals, we cannot rewrite our history. What happened is what has happened. Simple. The facts are the facts. If we grew up with a depressed parent as our primary caregiver—with all that entails—we can't change that fact. It is what it is, and it's what we have to work with.

Of course, you may already understand this intellectually and rationally, but on an emotional level, it's easy to cling to the fantasy that the past can be redone. The good news is that although the facts cannot be altered, your perception of the past and the story that you tell yourself about it can indeed change, as you will see.

FACT AND FICTION IN YOUR OWN HISTORY

There are always two parts to what we recount of our own life experiences. One part is fact, and one part is fiction. The first part, the facts, are the things that happened. *My mother was depressed* is an example of a fact. It has no value judgment. It is not good or bad. It doesn't mean anything other than it occurred. With these facts, there is no embellishment.

The other part, the fictions—the stories—are the things that we tell ourselves about what happened. For example, you may tell yourself, *I wasn't a very good son or daughter, and that is why my mother was depressed.* Here is where we run into all sorts of meaning making. We take a fact—albeit, one very close to home—and turn it into something other than just a clear statement about what happened. We turn the event into something that is either good or bad—assign some judgment to it—and can continue to do so for the rest of our lives in a less-than-conscious way. Really, most of what we're doing throughout each and every day is making up stories and judging.

Being Honest with Yourself

Note that it's important not to confuse truth telling with affirmations. The idea with affirmations is that all we have to do is repeat something for long enough in the right way to make it come true. But will it? Affirmations have a long track record of use among a wide array of people. From those seeking wealth and fame to those wanting to be healed of cancer, the usage of affirmations has been widely touted.

Unfortunately, the notion that we can make something happen if we just say that it will is either wishful thinking or plain old bull. We cannot lie to ourselves, over and over again, without repercussions. Yes, being positive—receiving support and encouragement—is vital. At the same time, if we let that positivity become delusional, to the point that we are seduced into the notion that all we have to do to feel better or change things is repeat a certain series of words over and over again, then we are just parroting ourselves.

Being honest is an important value to uphold. If you are struggling, it is important to acknowledge the reality of that struggle and not merely gloss over those struggles with word frosting.

It just won't work to ignore the truth of your immediate experience. For example, imagine yourself going to see your primary family physician. Your doctor walks into the room and, instead of being honest about the ache that brought you there, you say to the doctor, "I am great! Never felt better. I feel like a million bucks! I have never been so happy and healthy in all of my life."

Your doctor would probably ask, "Then why are you here?"

Our healing journey, as children of depressed parents, requires us to be honest. At the same time, that does not mean we should spin in circles with negativity. That won't help us get anywhere but farther down and more stuck. The path to healing is to be truthful with ourselves so we can move through it and beyond.

Accepting Your Experience

The next exercise will help you to become acquainted with the practice of telling the truth about your experience. It may be uncomfortable at first, especially if you have a habit of ignoring or glossing over how you feel or putting your own feelings on the back burner for the sake of others.

Exercise: Honest and Supportive Truth Telling

Below are some examples of how you can reframe some of your negative and harmful thoughts in an affirmative and honest way. On the left side are some self-destructive thoughts that are common to children of the depressed. On the right side are examples of how to interpret your experience in a more positive and compassionate way.

Self-Destructive Thought	Compassionate Thought
I'm not lovable.	*I am loved, even by those who are too ill to show me their love.*
I'm not worth much.	*Just trying my best makes me worthy.*
I can't control my anger.	*I'm learning healthy ways to express myself.*
I'll never be happy.	*I look forward to enjoying my life.*
Everyone depends on me.	*Others need to learn to take care of themselves.*
I have to perform well.	*I count, no matter what.*
My needs shouldn't matter.	*My first responsibility is to myself.*
I'm strong. I don't need anybody.	*Allowing others to support me is itself a strength, not a weakness.*
If I'm not perfect, then I'm a failure.	*I'm proud of myself that I'm doing the best I can at this time.*
"I have to seem okay on the outside, so no one will know who or how I really am."	"I'm finding the help I need, so the inside of me can match the outside."

Write down some of your own self-destructive thoughts, and then come up with corresponding compassionate thoughts that are a more accurate reflection of yourself and the life you are moving toward. You can use the space provided here or write in your journal.

_____

_____

_____

_____

_____

You may encounter some resistance with reframing some of the fictions that have taken root in you over the years. This is a typical reaction at the beginning of healing. If you had a strong emotional reaction to some of the examples in this exercise, these examples may be a clue to where your deepest personal fictions lie. Take a moment to step back to get some perspective on why you may encounter such resistance. If it feels right, you can write down the reasons why you resist doing this exercise or why you believe a certain painful thought is true in your case.

The purpose of this practice is to increase your own awareness of the stories that you tell yourself. The goal, as you move forward, is to notice the difference between when you are telling the truth and when you may be glossing over your experience and diminishing your truth, perhaps for the sake of others.

COGNITIVE BEHAVIORAL THERAPY

Moving through life assuming that whatever we think or feel must be true can present us with several problems. If we never question our thoughts and the feelings they can arouse in us, and it happens that those thoughts are not in fact true, we end up living a lie and not knowing it or ever attempting to correct it.

Cognitive behavioral therapy has become a popular approach to dealing with mental illness and has proven to be effective in treating phobias, anxiety, and depression. The main emphasis when using CBT is to begin to question what is referred to in this therapy as *automatic thoughts*. These are the thoughts that come to you as easily as breathing, thoughts that occur automatically through years of repetition and reinforcement. A belief is simply a thought that has occurred over and over again.

Of course, unless and until we begin to pay attention to our thoughts, we won't know what they are and what they are saying about us or about life in general. A common assumption is that we are having these thoughts consciously and that they are reflective of the truth. It is therefore easy to believe our thoughts, even if our beginning to question them is the first sign of freedom we have known in a long time.

As you can begin to sense, there is a place for some healthy doubt and skepticism about your thoughts. Rather than believing them to be true—and therefore having your behavior dictated by unexamined thoughts—you can begin to question them. Certain *cognitive distortions*, or distortions in your thinking, may be the result of your being a child of a depressed parent.

Sometimes asking the simple question, "Hmm—am I sure that is true?" can be enough to challenge unhelpful thoughts. We don't need to interrogate our thoughts ruthlessly. We don't need to badger and belittle ourselves for having such automatic thoughts. We all have them. Just a light sense of curiosity and inquisitiveness can be more than enough to get the work done here. It can even be fun and exhilarating. I have seen people begin to question and doubt thoughts that they never had reason to believe they could question and doubt, and suddenly an amazing sense of light, wonder, hope, and freedom comes over and through them.

Just imagine what a relief it must be to suddenly realize that a terrible thought is not true. For example, you may have always thought, *I am no good. No one will ever love me. I am not worthy of being loved.* Then you suddenly realize it's not true. It's as if you were sentenced to certain and impending doom and now are being given a reprieve from certain thoughts that have crippled you for many years.

WRITING A NEW CHAPTER

While it is important to know that what happens to us when we are children can shape and mold us, having an impact on who we become later in life, it is equally important, if not more so, to know that our perception about what has already happened is not final. We can write new chapters. We don't need to continue to repeat the same story, with the same ending, and have that become our norm. Nor do we need to let cognitive distortions go on determining the way we think and feel about ourselves and about life in general.

Have you ever read a book, or seen a movie, in which some surprise twist left you stunned, in total shock and disbelief? Maybe it was *Sixth Sense*, starring Bruce Willis, or perhaps *The Crying Game* with Forest Whitaker. Maybe you remember reading a mystery and you thought you knew what was going to happen, only to have the plot twist unexpectedly and catch you by total surprise. You thought you knew what the outcome would be. You thought you knew what was going on. Then something else happened.

Can you be open to surprises in your life? Can you be open to the unexpected? Can you be open to the possibility that what has already happened in your life doesn't have to flow toward an obvious ending? That you are a song whose final note has not yet been sung? That you are a movie whose ending you don't already know?

Of course you can, and if you haven't begun already, you will start to question the automatic assumptions behind some of the thoughts that arise in your mind.

Learning How to Pay Attention

Paying attention is important. It is how we notice things. It is how we learn. It is how we pick things up from others. As the child of a depressed parent, you learned how to pay attention to your depressed mother or father. You probably did so because you wanted to know if your parent was okay or needed anything from you. Or you wanted to know if your parent was going to be irritable that day. Maybe you had to pay attention to know when to hide and steer clear of your parent.

Paying attention to others is not something that comes hard to children of depressed parents. It is, in many ways, a survival skill. We pay attention a lot and often too much.

The price of paying attention to others—because we grew up in a household where we became acclimated, habituated, or conditioned to doing so—often comes at the expense of knowing how to pay attention to ourselves.

Taking all (or nearly all) of your cues from others about how to be in the world—being motivated by external cues—can be a real issue for children of depressed parents. Over time, what seems to happen is that children of a depressed parent often sacrifice their own internal cues so that they can attend to their depressed mother or father. In your own case, it may mean that you dismiss your feelings for the sake of what those around you may be feeling. That is, you habitually treat your own thoughts and feelings as less important than the thoughts and feelings of your depressed parent, your friends, or others in your life.

The depressed parent's thoughts and feelings become primary, and those of the children and the spouse are treated as less important. And no one says this out loud, which is a key to this situation. Your depressed mother or father didn't have to say, "My overwhelming feelings of helplessness are more important than anything you can think or feel as a child." Or "If you hadn't done that stupid thing, I wouldn't be yelling at you right now!" That was unnecessary, although sometimes they may have said it. When you are living with a depressed person, their feelings and moods dominate the household, and everyone who lives in the household takes their cues from this dominating depressive energy.

Finding Your Self

Growing up reacting and responding to a parent inverts the natural and desired parent-child relationship, in which the parent responds to the child. In some ways, the child becomes the parent, and the parent becomes the child. "How is Mom today?" becomes more than just the normal, passing inquiry of a typical child. It becomes, instead, a central question. The child becomes the one who is worried and concerned for the well-being of the parent. And while many children adapt quite well to these novel circumstances, it goes without saying that having to worry about and care about the mental health of your mother or father at such a young age can leave a lasting impression. Maybe even a scar or two, somewhere deep inside.

What is the cost of having to give up a proper focus on your own young self so early in life, before you have had a chance to fully form your sense of self in relation to the world? More significantly, what happens to you when your self is formed as the caregiver of the family, and this happens at such a young age? Do you become more responsible than you should have to be? Does it feel like the weight of the world is upon your shoulders, because you have this notion that someone in your family has to hold it all together, because Mom or Dad can't?

What does this mean for you later in life? What does this mean for your adult relationships? Do you wake up one day full of resentment and bitterness, because you feel like you have had to watch out for everyone your whole life when no one has ever watched out for you? Perhaps, most importantly, have you come to believe that you are capable of taking care of everyone else but yourself?

As children of the depressed, we typically end up feeling the need to sacrifice ourselves to focus on our depressed parents. When parents are debilitated in such a way that they cannot attend to their children and be present for them, it creates a template for children so that they then have no sense of how to attend to their own developing personhood. Perhaps it is no surprise, then, that one of the more important tasks for you now is to learn how to attend to yourself, to be present to your own experience rather than looking outside. Robyn, whom you met earlier, put it best: "Don't expect to get the parenting that you wanted. You have to take care of yourself now. Come to peace with what you feel you didn't get from your parents, what they did or didn't do. They're not going to be able to give you what you wanted when you were little. I love my parents and accept them for who they are. I'm in charge of my life now and of giving myself what I need when I need it."

Robyn is correct. Your depressed parent was not able to give you what you needed all the time. Maybe you seldom received the kind of attention that you needed, that every child wants and deserves. But now you need to attend to yourself.

Attending to Yourself

While it may not be easy or familiar to attend to yourself and validate your own experience—because you may have no template or model for doing so—it is essential for your healing.

There is just no way around it. You cannot heal yourself by losing yourself in others and their concerns. You cannot heal yourself by doing what your depressed parent modeled for you, which was to ignore your needs and devalue your experience. In fact, the only way you can truly heal yourself is by providing yourself with what your depressed parent could not offer you as a child—focused attention on your self, including your dreams, aspirations, fears, follies, and fantasies.

The French philosopher and mathematician Blaise Pascal said, "All of humanity's problems stem from man's inability to sit quietly in a room alone." For a child of a depressed parent, this can be especially true. After all, what are you faced with when sitting in a small room by yourself? What is there to distract you, to divert your attention, to occupy your time, to swallow up your days and hours? Nothing, right? No one else to attend to. There is only you. And if you were never given the kind of stable presence and focus from your mother or father as a child that every child needs—to one degree or another—then sitting in a room by yourself may be more than a little daunting. In fact, for some it can be downright hellish. "I dread being alone with my head" is the gist of it.

Nonetheless, learning how to attend to your own experience is critical. It may make you very uncomfortable at first. It is probably going to feel unfamiliar. Maybe you have never done it in your entire life. Maybe you have led your whole life seeking to be distracted from yourself by involving and investing yourself in the lives and circumstances of others. Maybe you have bounced from one relationship to another. Maybe you have tried to be a saint, always helping others. Maybe you don't think you are that important.

The habit of devaluing and diminishing ourselves is more common than you may think it is. You are doing it every time you say anything like "Oh, I am not worth bothering with.

I prefer to focus on other people." Or "There is nothing inside of me. There is really no point. I'd rather just do stuff." If this sounds like you, the next exercise will help you learn to attend to your own needs.

Exercise: Caring for the Child in You

Imagine a child. If you have your own children, reflect on how you hold them, on how much you love them. If you have no children of your own, think about how you would listen to your nephew or niece or to the child of someone you know. Then, begin to feel yourself as this child—one who has thoughts and feelings, who looks at the world in unique and wonderful ways. Feel yourself as this child who needs others to listen—really listen. Feel how important it is to this child to be appreciated, and that the only way that this child can feel appreciated is by others listening. Feel how much love flows to you as this child.

Now, think about the kind of mood you would create for a child you love. Would you ever brush the child aside? Would you ever dismiss a child you cared about? Would you ever unwittingly diminish and devalue your child by disregarding experiences that he or she shared with you?

You can do this exercise whenever you notice yourself diminishing your own needs. The next step in healing is to turn your attention back to the process of how you routinely think about the past and the stories that you tell yourself. If your thoughts are distorted and self-destructive, then you need some new ways of approaching these thoughts whenever you have them. The next section will give you a new tool to help you address these thoughts whenever they arise.

HEALING YOUR THINKING WITH SCARS

Whenever you catch yourself having distorted and self-destructive thoughts, you can use the SCARS technique, which I developed over years of working with people who grew up with depressed parents. All you have to do is remember the handy acronym SCARS, which stands for the following:

Stop!

Congratulate yourself.

Apologize to yourself.

Replace the destructive distortion.

Smile.

The SCARS acronym helps us to remember both the steps and their healing power. It is a wonderful reminder of the truth that as human beings, we all have the inherent capacity to heal.

The SCARS technique helps you move to that place where the open wounds in your thinking (and feeling) no longer bleed, are no longer sore and tender, and no longer present you with a risk of infection.

It should be obvious to you that time does not heal all wounds. That's why you're reading this book. Deep psychological and emotional wounds won't go away by themselves any more than a deep physical wound will vanish without proper treatment. You need proven and effective strategies and techniques for treating your psychological and emotional wounds if you want to stop the hurt. If all you are doing is waiting for your life to change for the better, you are being unrealistic. Instead, try embracing the healing SCARS technique.

Step 1: Stop!

The first step in treating your psychological and emotional wounds is to stop. Just stop. Stop the bleeding. Stop reopening the old wound by picking at it. If you are not yet healed, then you need to stop whatever it is that is preventing effective healing from taking place and a scar from forming. Of course, you need to pay attention to your own thoughts or actions that are keeping you from healing. You need to notice when you are having negative and harmful thoughts about yourself and stop them. Such self-destructive thoughts keep your internal wounds open and fresh. Each time a self-destructive thought goes unchallenged—each time you don't stop the thought when you find yourself starting to think it—you are once again reopening an old wound.

If you are going to be realistic, then you need to stop badgering yourself with the distortions that arose during the trying times of your youth—the times when you did the best you could in formulating your experience as a child with a depressed parent—and you need to stop re-creating the traumas and trials of the past because it is either what you think you deserve or all you have ever known.

One more word on stopping. Applying a little pressure is often all it takes to stop a physical wound from bleeding. Likewise, applying some gentle but firm pressure against your self-destructive thoughts may be all it will take to remedy the hurt inside.

Step 2: Congratulate Yourself

Congratulations! Noticing when you are having self-harmful thoughts and then stopping—even temporarily—is a monumental step. If the first step is stopping what undermines your own native healing process, then the second step is congratulating yourself for doing it. It is so important to congratulate yourself at this juncture. First, because it is an indication that you have begun to gain self-awareness about some of the destructive distortions, damaging fictions, lies, and stories you've told about yourself. Second, because you may have a tendency to shame and humiliate yourself even further when you catch yourself involuntarily being hard on yourself. Kicking yourself for kicking yourself probably comes very naturally to you. This step will eliminate that. Yes, congratulations are in order.

Step 3: Apologize to Yourself

After congratulating yourself, you need to apologize to yourself: *I am sorry for picking on you. You didn't deserve that.*

If you have any reservations about this, please consider what would happen if you unwittingly discovered yourself picking at someone else's open wound. Would you think that was okay? Of course not! Yet we often pick at our own wounds in involuntary and unconscious ways. And some of those patterns of behavior will continue until we stop them, congratulate ourselves for noticing what we were doing, apologize to ourselves, and then...

Step 4: Replace the Destructive Distortion

Imagine you are a nurse and you see one of your patients picking at an open wound. What would you say? After saying, "Stop it—that's not good for you," you might suggest some ways to assist the patient's own native healing process. Maybe you would show the patient how to apply a soothing salve.

Whenever a destructive distorted thought arises, your job is to replace it with a supportive and helpful thought that facilitates healing. You took this step earlier in the chapter when you looked at the self-destructive thoughts of your own personal story and did the exercise of replacing them with compassionate thoughts. Again, we end up picking at ourselves and undermining our own potential because we have come to believe that our cognitive distortions are true, and no one has yet shown, or told, us anything different. If you need assistance with this step, review the earlier exercise and apply the same sort of reframing as often as necessary, which initially may be a lot.

Step 5: Smile

Smile. Each time you stop, congratulate, apologize, and replace—when you are dealing with a distorted idea about who you are and what your worth is—you are taking one more step toward a happier and healthier world for yourself and for anyone whom your existence touches on a daily basis. So smile. Smile because your wounds will slowly heal. Smile because you are learning how to congratulate yourself for the things you are learning and the things you have already lived through. Smile because you know how important it is to apologize to yourself when you catch yourself being hard on yourself, just like you'd smile at anyone else you love if they did the same. Smile because you are taking away the momentum of destructive cognitive distortions in your life, one step at a time. Smile because you are uprooting what undermines you and replacing it with what uplifts you. Smile because this SCARS exercise reminds you of what you have been through and the healing that has already taken place. Smile because your scars are telling a story whose healthier chapters are still being written. So go ahead and smile.

However, if you don't feel like smiling, give yourself time. And please...please do not use the fact that you don't feel like smiling as another reason to think you are lacking what's necessary or yet another reason to beat yourself up for not making the grade.

One final word needs to be said about the SCARS technique. You may have thought, *I don't want any scars on me. Scars are a bad thing.* While few people want to have scars or be scarred for life, having a scar is a lot better than having an open, festering wound. Physically, scar tissue isn't exactly the same as the tissue replaced, but it is totally functional and keeps the body whole, healthy, and together.

The same is true with the kind of emotional and psychological scars that will form over the long-term festering wounds that have accrued to you as the child of a depressed parent. After a while, you will rarely notice the scar or be tempted to poke it, prod it, and see what's underneath it. If you do prod deeply enough, you may indeed resurrect remnants of what hurt you—how you weren't properly supported by your depressed parent, how you believed in the distorted view of who you were that was reflected back to you, and so on. From time to time, we're all tempted to go back and relive what hurt us most. If you find yourself doing this, return to the SCARS technique and stop!

Over time, as you become more whole and healthy, you will find this urge diminishing. Your emotional and psychological scars will be just emotional and psychological scars, artifacts of the healing process and nothing more. Over time, in fact, these scars may nearly completely fade away, becoming a mere memory of something you have triumphed over, symbols and reminders of how you survived.

LOOKING BACK

You have come a long way already. Before you continue, I would like to congratulate you on coming this far. As someone who truly understands this area, I want you to know just how profound this all is. Yes, you may still be struggling. Yes, you may still have doubts and reservations. You probably still have some unanswered questions. This is all quite normal. It's fine. You are doing great.

So take a deep breath and look over your shoulder at all you have come through, at all you have come to better understand, at all the steps on your journey that have led you here. Look back at the story you were living when you didn't think there was any other story to live or when you thought you knew how the ending would look. Look back and see all the little triumphs and trials along the way, and then gather yourself. There is more of your life to be written and to be lived. Congratulations.

KEY POINTS

- The significant events that take place in our lives form and shape the stories we make up about ourselves. There are the facts, and then there is what we say, think, and believe about what happened—the stories. Learning to separate the two will change your life forever.

- The burden of untold tales can be suffocating and debilitating.

- We cannot change the facts of our lives without being dishonest with ourselves and with those who share our world. We can, however, positively and honestly reframe our perceptions about the facts so that their truthfulness is more helpful to us.

- Scars are both a sign of injury and an indication of our innate healing power. You can use the SCARS technique to stop picking at yourself with your thoughts and begin replacing longtime open wounds with healthy scars, which will ultimately lead to the happiness you desire.

CHAPTER 5

Feeling Better by Feeling More

Our feelings are a huge factor in determining our sense of well-being. It is our feelings that we thrive on, crave, and resist. Feelings and emotions like love and compassion can represent the pinnacle of life and all that makes life worth living, just as other feelings and emotions, like grief and despair, sometimes make it seem as though life is not worth living at all. Yet being able to fully access our feelings and emotions, whether difficult or not, is important to our mental and physical health.

This chapter will look more closely at the role that your feelings play in your life. It will help you reflect on what you were encouraged or allowed to feel as a child and what you were not encouraged or allowed to feel. It will also help you learn how to parent your emotional self, so that you can more fully access and accept buried or difficult feelings.

THINKING AND FEELING

To begin, if we are honest with ourselves, it doesn't take long to surmise that our *thinking* self and our *feeling* self are closely related. They are sometimes indistinguishable. We may believe that they are separate, but just as our head is inseparable from our body, so, too, are our thoughts and feelings connected.

We cannot separate the thoughts that arise in our minds from the feelings that course through our bodies. This means that it is virtually impossible for us to have self-destructive thoughts and not feel self-destructive. Similarly, it is impossible to feel self-destructive and not have self-destructive thoughts arising in our minds. Where we have one, we also will find the other.

Which Came First?

It's like the old chicken and egg quandary. We don't know which comes first, thoughts or feelings, but we do know that both exist. And for us to be healthy, we need to take both our thoughts and our feelings into account.

Chapter 4 looked at the tremendous role our thoughts play in our sense of well-being. Likewise, if we want to have joyous and contented thoughts arising within us, then we need to find ways to feel joyous and content. Since you are a child of depressed parents, odds are these feelings aren't easy for you to access. Because you did not receive the best kinds of support and encouragement, at least not consistently, having access to your full emotional self may be difficult for you, but it is something that you can work on.

Learning to Self-Regulate

One of the most fundamental things parents can do for children is to help them learn how to regulate, accept, and effectively deal with their feelings. Fully present parents do this for their children. They provide emotional nurturing, in addition to providing a home in which to live, food to eat, and a bed to sleep in. But children of the depressed often miss out.

What were you shown about how to deal with frustration and disappointment when you were a child? What did your parents show you—and, in the showing, teach you—about how to deal with not always getting your way? How did your parents model resilience for you, or did they model it at all? Maybe your parents modeled the opposite: ways of not bouncing back, ways of not recovering from disappointment. Maybe your depressed parent was not always effective and present in demonstrating to you skillful ways for dealing with life's inevitable disappointments.

Exercise: Revisit Your Past

Take a moment now to reflect on the ways your depressed parent showed you how to deal with pain and suffering, hurt and disappointment, loss and failure. Did you feel held as a child when you were hurt or when you were suffering? Did you feel that your mother or father was present for you? How were you treated when you came to your parent with your hurt? Did your parent allow it? Receive it? Or were you given the message that your hurt was unwelcome?

When you cried, did one or both of your parents soothe you? Were you able to openly express your frustration and disappointment, or were your attempts to do this either ignored or brushed aside?

How did your depressed parent help you manage other feelings? Looking back, what—if anything—did you learn about how to work with a sense of disappointment, an illness, a loss, or difficult situations in general? What were the ways you were taught about how to deal with what was hard for you? For instance, if you were upset about something that happened at school, and this led to you feeling sad, was this something that you could bring to your mother or father to discuss? Were feelings, in general, something that you could talk about with your depressed parent? Was your parent too absorbed in his or her own feelings to attend to yours?

If so, what message did that send to you about what your feelings meant, and how the world would (or would not) receive them?

You may want to take a moment to write in the space below, or you can write in your journal, about your experience as a child.

_____

_____

_____

_____

_____

Obviously no parent or family is perfect. Not even that family that lives down the street from you. You know the ones—whose car is always clean, whose grass is always freshly mowed, and whose trash is always taken out early and appears to have been carefully sorted and prepared for the curb. The best you can hope for is a parent who is the right one for you.

If you were the child of a depressed parent, though, odds are that things might not have been quite right enough for you. You might not have had the kind of secure attachment that sets the stage for emotional well-being and even general good health later in life. As a reminder, if you do not experience a relatively successful attachment in your early development—one that feels secure, consistent, and stable—then you are less likely to achieve successful emotional attachments later in life (see chapter 3). Later, this chapter will offer some specific ways to address issues of insecure attachment; but for now, here's a story showing how such insecure attachment develops.

■ Rebecca's Story

Rebecca grew up in a home that was, by all outward appearances, idyllic. Her father was a successful lawyer. Her mother, Donna, was heavily involved in various community-oriented volunteer and fundraising efforts. These efforts made everyone believe that Rebecca's mother was a buoyant spirit who had a bottomless well from which to give. But for Rebecca, who was an only child, this was not at all the case.

Donna suffered from postpartum depression after giving birth to Rebecca. She struggled mightily with her emotions as a new mother. In fact, she dreamt of—and longed for—the day when she could once again be out in the community networking and offering her services to those in need. Doing community work made her feel competent. She knew she was at least good at those things, and she felt like a failure as a mother. As much as she hated to admit it, since becoming a mother, Donna felt horribly inadequate.

Since her husband provided the income and spent so much time at work, Donna felt like the responsibility for providing emotional support and nourishment to Rebecca was all on her. To make matters worse, Rebecca's parents had moved from the small town where they'd met to a city where they didn't have the solid support that family often provides when a new child comes along.

As time went on, raising Rebecca became a daily obligation that fell more and more on Donna's shoulders. She sought professional help for her depression but could not find anyone who could give her the support she required. As her depression grew, she became increasingly isolated, overwhelmed, and resentful.

Ashamed of what she was actually feeling, Donna did her best to put on a happy face whenever others were around.

In secret, though, Donna struggled to get out of bed each morning. Rebecca's cries grated on her nerves, wore her down, and became a constant reminder of how alone, hopeless, and even doomed she felt in her life as a stay-at-home mom. Breastfeeding was not the warm, fuzzy experience that so many mothers said it could be. Certainly not for Donna and her daughter.

To compound matters, Donna started to feel increasingly guilty about her feelings of being burdened as the sole caregiver for her child. When she would meet with her friends or speak with her family several states away, she would say, "Everything is great!" even as she knew in her heart of hearts that everything was not great. What she thought was supposed to be the happiest time of her life had become the most miserable. Knowing this made Donna even more miserable, something she allowed herself to feel or express only when no one else was looking.

As a child, Rebecca could not help but pick up on her mother's feelings through her mom's behavior. Donna was anxious when she held Rebecca, so her muscles were tense, her facial expression was stern, and her voice was curt. And Donna's depression continued well into Rebecca's childhood, having a big impact on her daughter. Rebecca grew up anxious about her own feelings and where to go with them. It was as if her emotional life had become this potent storm, one that was always on the verge of spiraling out of control. Rebecca did her best to keep everything together and stay in control. If what it took was pretending that she didn't have any emotions, then that is what she did.

Postpartum depression is not nearly as rare as you would believe, and the impacts on children of the depressed are real. Think about it. If Donna had not become depressed after Rebecca's birth, how might Rebecca's relationship to her own emotions have differed? Imagine a scenario in which Rebecca cried as a child, because she was hungry, frightened, or teething, and her mother immediately responded to her discomfort with full attention and love. Imagine a scenario where Rebecca experienced suffering as an infant, and her mother naturally soothed her child with song or soft stroking. Imagine a scenario where Donna consistently sent the message that whenever Rebecca experienced discomfort, it was okay, that when she suffered, she would be treated with kindness, that when she was tired and irritable, she would be given a soft place to lie down, and that when she was hungry, she would be fed with nourishing food.

In fact, most depressed mothers try extra hard to give what is needed to their babies, but it often feels like an acting job. These moms try to push through their depression, so they can be there for their babies the way they feel they ought to be. Trust me, it's exhausting—I've been there. And even if they didn't pick up on the depression as babies, children whose parent's depression persists, as it often can, may eventually be affected negatively.

Exercise: Reimagine Your Past

Now imagine a scenario where you didn't have to run from, hide, or disown any feelings you had, because you were consistently offered the message, as a child, that your needs were fine and would be met and that your cries of suffering would always be answered.

Imagine that when you cried as a child, someone always came. And when that someone came, they came ready to offer you comfort and ways of addressing your needs. As a child, you would have thereby received the message that any pain and suffering—

that any difficult emotions and feelings that arose within you—would have been regularly answered and lovingly responded to.

Allow yourself to sit with the feelings that come up. You also can write down some of your thoughts in the space below or in your journal, if this helps you reimagine the past.

_____

_____

_____

_____

The child you imagined in this exercise would have received good parenting; but again, when someone has a depressed parent, such parenting is often lacking, no matter how much love the parent feels for the child. Someone who is depressed can be physically present and yet not really there for others. This suggests that we don't need to have been physically abandoned to have experienced abandonment as children of the depressed. Our parents could have literally been with us every single day of our childhood and yet not been fully present emotionally, attending to our rightful needs and development.

As discussed already, and as you probably know all too well, depression has an insidious way of making people emotionally unavailable. Depression is a lot like a deep well. It is isolating and all-consuming, and it has a way of separating people from those around them. When I was depressed, there were many occasions when I was surrounded by people who loved me yet could not reach me—I still felt alone at the bottom of that well, and desperately sad.

I did my very best with my children, but my depression guaranteed that we felt disconnected from each other. Children want nothing more than to stand shining in the light of their parents' loving attention. Depression in parents robs children and also often deprives the parents of a bonding experience. Your parents may not have been able to see you as the person you really were—since depression has such a distorting effect on perception—and you might not have had the experience of really being seen. Depression typically becomes like a wall that prevents this deeper emotional connection. It impairs the secure attachment that so much in our later lives rests upon.

HOW YOU FEEL TODAY

If you did not have the kind of secure attachment that comes with good parenting, you may experience debilitating emotional states, such as anxiety, later on in life. This does not mean that others—those who had secure attachments to their parents in early childhood—do not experience anxiety; they most certainly do. What it does mean is that the kind of insecure attachment that affects and colors the life of a child with a depressed parent will, in all likelihood, lead that child—and later that adult—to wrestle with difficult emotional states, such as anxiety, more regularly and intensely than other people.

Earlier, you looked at some of the obstacles that will likely present themselves to you on your healing journey. One such obstacle is anxiety, specifically the sense that things are "not going to be okay." As is often the case with children of depressed parents, you may experience a near constant low-level anxiety. The distress and anxiety of your early childhood was stored and carried. Even if it seems to disappear and go underground, it returns in those specific situations that mimic those times when you felt anxious and were not properly and effectively soothed and reassured as a child. If your needs were chronically unmet—the need for emotional connection, the need for parental recognition, the need for consistently compassionate responses to your distress as a child—then all of that anxiety about your needs not being met has been carried forward.

If your parents are unable to show up and offer you the kind of support you need, because they are in the throes of the debilitating illness that is depression, then you can't discover who you are or can become. To a greater or lesser degree, your development became arrested and distorted. If the reality of the situation is not lucidly explained to you in a sufficient timeframe, you begin to believe that those distortions are who you really are. It is like being at a carnival and going into the Fun House of Mirrors, where you stand before a mirror that makes you look all stretched out and wavy, or two feet tall and eight feet wide. What you see and feel is not who you are. The distortion is not because you are deformed. The distortion is the result of an environment that does not reflect back to you a true image and sense of who you were and who you are.

BELIEVING THE LIE IS FEELING THE LIE

When we are children and are not offered realistic reflections of who we truly are—because our parents have a debilitating condition, such as depression, that does not allow them to reflect back to us who we are in an accurate and realistic way—we don't laugh or giggle about it. The Fun House of Mirrors becomes the Haunted House of Horrors that induces stress, anxiety, and terror within us. The postpartum depression of Rebecca's mom distorted her mom's perception of Rebecca as a young child. Rebecca therefore grew up feeling like she was a problem, difficult, and needy.

As children, inaccurate reflections mirror back to us lies and distortions that we often come to believe are accurate depictions of ourselves—because we don't know any better, and no one tells us any better. This is how seeing ourselves through the eyes of a depressed parent can lead us to feeling like we are that which we in fact are not. We look like we might be a monster, so we begin to feel like we might be a monster.

RE-PARENTING OUR EMOTIONAL SELVES

Chapter 4 introduced a technique called SCARS, which can be used to address and correct some of the distortions that can come to dominate the thinking of children of the depressed. Just as there is a technique that can help you clear up some of the distortions in your thinking, there is a technique that—again, with practice—can help you clear up some of the distortions in your feelings. What you can do is re-parent your emotional self, offering yourself the parenting that you never had. In this way, you will learn how to acknowledge and accept the full range of your emotional life, which is necessary to heal.

Again, odds are that when you experienced the presence of difficult emotions as a child, there were times when you had nowhere to go with them. Your parent was unable to meet you where you were or show understanding of what you were feeling. In this way, you were never shown how to effectively hold and make sense of your various emotions. Maybe some emotions seemed okay to have. Maybe others did not. As a result, a portion of your emotional identity may have been deemed unacceptable or unworthy, wrong or bad, ugly or foreign, vile or wicked. Maybe you could not be angry. Maybe you could not be distressed at all, and were forced to wear a happy face all the time. Perhaps you had to be stoic day in and day out and keep a stiff upper lip. Or maybe you were never allowed to be enthusiastic and excited about events, because your home was dark and the mood of your home was designed to match the mood of your depressed parent.

Really, any emotion could have been cut off. In my experience, it is totally dependent on the subtle and not-so-subtle messages that parents send to their children all the time about what is okay or not okay to feel. The problem with this is well known and indisputable: we cannot deny, dismiss, denounce, or dismember ourselves emotionally without serious and debilitating repercussions.

Exercise: Which Emotions Weren't Allowed?

Reflect carefully on each emotion listed here. What voices, pictures, or feelings come to mind when you think of having each emotion as a child? How do you remember or imagine your parents reacting? Were any of them frowned upon or reacted to in any negative way? Were they ignored? Use the space provided (or your journal) to write about a time when you were feeling these emotions (or imagine a time when that emotion would naturally have surfaced for you as a child).

Angry _____

Frustrated _____

Excited _____

Upset _____

Sad _____

Happy _____

Other _____

Now ask yourself how able you are today as an adult to express these emotions. If more thoughts are triggered, feel free to continue writing in your journal.

If you have discovered that certain emotions were unacceptable in your childhood, you can use this information as you learn to offer yourself the parenting that you may not have received as a child.

Considering Your Feelings

One could argue that the real issue is not the emotions themselves—whether they are anger, sadness, grief, loneliness, or despair. The issue is that so many of us don't know what to do with these difficult emotions when they arise. Not everyone understands the difference, though, at least not initially. The general tendency is to want to get rid of difficult emotions rather than change our relationship to them.

In other words, we need to look at *how* we can hold our emotions rather than whether we will hold them. We need to look at *where* we will go with them rather than whether we will go anywhere with them. We need to embrace all of our emotions rather than get rid of the more difficult ones while letting the others stick around.

The challenge with regard to your emotional self is much like any other challenge you might face. If you'd never learned to read because no one ever showed you how to read, that wouldn't mean you were stupid. It would instead mean that you were never properly educated. Reading, then, is a skill you pick up from others and learn how to do on your own. The same is true with respect to your emotions. There doesn't need to be any great complexity about this. Keep it simple.

Our emotions are a gift. Our emotions are responses to circumstances and situations around us. Even anger, upset, disappointment, and other challenging emotions are not bad. Ultimately, we need to become capable of a healthy emotional responsiveness to life. As the Zen proverb states, "When tired, sleep. When hungry, eat. When sitting, sit. When walking, walk." If we are upset, then we need to learn to allow ourselves to be upset. We also need to know how and when to move on when it is time to let the disappointment or sense of betrayal go.

Re-parenting Technique

You can use this re-parenting technique and carry it forward with you as you retrain your emotional self for greater well-being. It has three basic steps:

Tell yourself it's okay.

Hold yourself.

Promise that you will be there.

You can use these three steps right now or whenever a difficult emotion comes up. It will help you soothe yourself in a way that you were never soothed as a child. Over time, doing this exercise will ease the pain of difficult emotions and allow you to explore the whole range of human experience.

STEP 1: TELL YOURSELF IT'S OKAY

"It's okay." What powerful words these are. There is so much contained in this little statement. So much of the kind of support and encouragement that we all need is housed in these two little words.

It's okay to feel. It's okay to be sad. It's okay to be upset. It's okay to care. It's okay to be happy. It's okay if you experience sadness and disappointment. It's all normal.

Hearing that it's okay can be such a relief, especially if early in life you heard it was not okay and then believed that it was not okay for two, three, or four decades after that. It is like someone giving you a part of yourself back! *Maybe there is not as much wrong with me as I was led to believe. Maybe I am not the monster I thought I was when looking at myself in the twisted reflection of my parent's illness.*

Note: It's also okay if you still think it's not okay. If you've believed that it is unacceptable to feel a certain emotion for virtually all of your life, then you cannot expect this belief to be overthrown in an instant, just because you're now hearing that it's all right to feel this way. You may need to give yourself more time before you can accept that certain feelings are okay to have.

Remember that every time you chip away at an emotional distortion, you are moving one step closer to the truth—to your healed, happy, and whole self.

STEP 2: HOLD YOURSELF

Imagine a young girl who falls and hurts herself while playing on the sidewalk. Her knee is scraped, a little blood oozes out, and the girl screams, "Mommy! Daddy! Oww!" Her parents rush over to her, scoop her up and hold her, and tell her, "It's okay."

However, from the perspective of the little girl who is in pain, it doesn't feel okay! In fact, it feels very un-okay. But when her parents hold her—the adults who have had their own knees scraped in the past and know that the pain will go away—the child is reassured. Even if the child continues to scream in protest, "It's not okay!!!" her parents know that it will be fine and continue to reassure her. The child receives this message by being held: *Yes, it hurts in the moment. Yes, it will take some time for the wound to heal. No, this is not fun. Yes, the pain that you feel right now can be overwhelming. No, Mommy is not going to let you go. Yes, Daddy is going to stay with you right here and hold you until you feel better. It's okay. It really is.*

If a parent is consistent in helping a child move through what is painful and difficult, the child will eventually believe what the parent says. The child still experiences the pain of the wounded knee and will still shed tears. Yet somewhere deep within that child, an unshakeable internal knowing will blossom that says, "Yes...it really will be okay."

If you did not have the kind of consistent parenting that offered you a sense that "It's okay," or if you heard the opposite, it is not too late. Your parents may not have been able to offer what was best for you back then, but the past is no excuse for not offering yourself what you need, or what is best for you, right now.

You can offer yourself the kind of holding, or soothing, that you didn't receive when you first experienced a difficult or intense emotion. *Holding yourself* does not necessarily have to be a physical act, although you can feel free to literally hug yourself. For this exercise, holding yourself can mean emotionally supporting yourself in any way that works for you.

You don't need to continue to shun your feelings or numb yourself to them. By more and more proactively allowing your emotions to be okay—even the hard and upsetting ones—you will slowly but surely, over time, recover your full self and your ability to access, allow, and work with the full spectrum of your emotions and feelings. In this way you will become whole— become all you can be—which will be a very good thing both for yourself and for those you love and care about.

STEP 3: PROMISE THAT YOU WILL BE THERE

The final step is a promise: the promise that you will always be there for yourself. That you will not abandon yourself. That you will not disappear on yourself. That you will not shun yourself for feeling a certain way. That you will go through thick and thin and do whatever it takes to show up for yourself. That you won't lie to make others happy. That you won't abandon your own emotions, just because they make someone else around you uncomfortable. This promise is a sacred vow, an eternal oath born of love and affection. You are promising to offer yourself what you truly deserve: your whole and complete emotional self, unconditionally.

YOUR JOURNEY

This chapter has taught you how to give yourself the parenting that you never had so that you can recover your emotional self. This recovery is a continuing journey, one that begins right now as you tell yourself that it's okay to feel how you feel, give yourself the reassurance that was missing from your childhood, and promise to remain emotionally present for yourself.

KEY POINTS

- Our thoughts and our feelings are inseparable. We think about what we feel, and our feelings coincide with our thoughts.

- Physical presence and emotional presence are not the same. Often, a depressed parent can be physically present but not emotionally present or involved.

- If your depressed parent was not able to help you experience some of the more difficult emotions that simply come as part of being alive, then it is likely that certain emotions will continue to present challenges for you as an adult.

- Distortions in your perception of yourself emotionally can be learned as a result of being a child of the depressed, just as distortions in your thinking can be learned.

- You can learn to re-parent your emotional self by working with your emotional and psychological wounds in a compassionate and attentive way. You can learn to be emotionally present both to and for yourself and for others.

CHAPTER 6

What to Do and What Not to Do on Your Journey of Healing

Chapters 4 and 5 looked closely at the role our thoughts and emotions play in our experience of life. Perhaps for the first time ever, you painstakingly dissected the nature of your thoughts, and you discovered that there is a crucial difference between fact (what happens) and fiction (the stories you tell yourself about what happened). Chapter 5 further explored the realm of feelings and the idea that it is not possible to heal and be wholly ourselves without also being whole emotionally. Together these chapters introduced the cognitive elements of cognitive behavioral therapy.

The next stage on your healing journey is to look at ways in which your behavior—what you do or don't do on a daily basis—may be shaped by the experience of growing up with a depressed parent. Examining your actions and inactions in life is an important part of the healing process. This chapter will show you that you have the power to correct actions that are no longer working for you, and this will help you make better choices.

B IS FOR BEHAVIOR

You may have been wondering where the B in CBT comes in. You may have noticed as you were reading this book that there has been precious little about actual behavior. Why so much talk about thoughts and feelings?

My aim in writing this book has been to approximate what it might be like to actually experience therapy and the positive results from therapy. The simple explanation, then, is that there is a desired sequence, or process, that needs to take place in a book like this. More specifically, this book has emphasized introspection and analysis first, because without an understanding of the underlying mechanisms at work in our lives, it's more difficult to experience the kinds of changes in our lives that will benefit us in the long run.

Making Gentle Corrections

Your next step is to look at the choices that you make every day so that you can begin to change behaviors that are not working for you. You may find this step to be a challenging one. Please remember to be gentle with yourself. Any time that you feel like you are not measuring up, or you are not doing enough, you can use the SCARS technique to challenge these thoughts. There is no need to judge yourself. No one is perfect. No one is infallible. We are not going to feel like we have gotten it right all the time. We all are going to fail on occasion—or at least feel like we have failed. But this does not make us failures.

As you change and grow—as you heal, and your wounds turn into scars—remember to be as gentle with yourself as you would be with a child learning to walk. If you stumble—and you will—it is not the end of the world. If you fall and slip back into old patterns and habits of thought and emotion, please know that it is okay. Take it as another opportunity to practice. It is not a sign that you are doomed or that you will never get it. It doesn't mean you are too old or too wounded. Find something to steady yourself upon and keep taking those baby steps toward healing.

Common Coping Behaviors

So what are the behaviors that you would like to change? Three common behaviors for children of the depressed are hiding the truth, suppressing our own needs and desires, and running away—each of which can be a response to living with a depressed parent. The next section will take a closer look at how each of these behaviors may play out in our adult lives and at how we can change unhelpful patterns.

BABY STEPS FOR ADULTS

You can take specific steps in your life to tell the truth, to assert yourself, and to be more present. These are all behaviors that reflect a whole and healthy individual. Even if you don't immediately get the sense that these steps will be relevant to your own situation, learning about them can still be helpful.

Tell the Truth

It may seem obvious. Just tell the truth, right? How hard can that be? Well, as you may know, it can be harder than you might suspect. As previously discussed, it may not have been acceptable to say what was wrong with your mother or father, or what was wrong in your home. Maybe you had to lie about why you could not have friends over. Maybe you had to lie each and every time you said, "I am fine." Maybe you grew up telling these self-protective lies so consistently that you never have really learned to fully tell the truth. After all, no one wants to think of themselves as a liar.

Children of the depressed typically tell lies for one of two reasons: because we want to protect our parents or because we are ashamed of our parents. In the first case, we may have lied to cover up for our parents. We didn't want anyone to think ill of them. If other people had known what was really going on, then those people might have looked down on them, and we couldn't allow that, because we loved our parents so much. The second possibility is that we lied to protect ourselves. The fear was that we would not be liked—that we would be judged negatively—if others discovered that our parents were depressed. The fear was that we would be ostracized and condemned if anyone found out.

Exercise: Why Did You Hide the Truth?

Ask yourself if you hid the truth sometimes from others when you were a child. If so, when did you do this? What did you say instead? When you lied, do you think you were trying to protect your parents or yourself? Take a moment to reflect on these questions and perhaps write in your journal if you like. Next ask yourself whether you continue to hide the truth today. When do you do this? Ask yourself whom you are trying to protect when you lie. Are you still trying to protect someone else? Are you trying to protect yourself? Do you still carry around shame from growing up with a depressed parent? Again, it may help to write down your thoughts in your journal.

Do you need to hide the truth about the past? Do you need to be ashamed any more? Absolutely not! In fact, you can come to better terms with the circumstances of your upbringing, regardless of what they may have been. This concept will be taken up again in chapter 10, where you will discover the special gifts and unique blessings that come only to those special few who are children of the depressed.

Learn to Be Assertive

Learning how to be assertive goes hand in hand with telling the truth. You can't do one without the other.

You may have difficulty with asserting your own needs and interests, because as a child, your own needs and wishes may have taken a back seat to the illness of your parent. If parental depression asserted itself in the household you were raised in, the odds are that asserting yourself was not a skill that you had an opportunity to regularly practice.

Compared to other people, we children of the depressed have an especially difficult time asserting ourselves. Swallowing our own desires and emotions, feelings, and wild ambitions may become the norm, the status quo. At times, even the thought of asserting ourselves may cause anxiety and nervousness. Sweaty palms, increased heart rate, short and shallow breathing—these are telltale signs that we are not in our comfort zone.

But you can learn to be more assertive in your life. You can learn to tell the truth. Later in this chapter, you will learn some new techniques for expressing yourself assertively without crossing the line into being dominating, or trying to control others.

Be Present

If shame, guilt, and a low sense of self-worth accompanied your upbringing, it only makes sense that you would have wanted to escape from what you sensed, on some level, was the source of those feelings. Children can use their imaginations as a sanctuary if their being is encroached upon in ways that make them want to go someplace else. While this can be a good thing—and is, perhaps, necessary for psychic survival and a child's ultimate well-being—some related challenges often arise. For one thing, this retreat-to-the-sanctuary mentality can result in our becoming too easily prone to want to flee any discomforting state or emotion, even as adults. It can lead to being somewhat unsteady in relationships. In effect, the risk is that we develop a history of avoidance.

The sense of powerlessness that came from being unable to truly help the one you loved the most may have rendered you immobile and passive. How could you assert yourself and have an impact as a child when your mother or father was so deeply debilitated by depression? How could you help them?

If you arrived at the conclusion that you could not help them—that nothing you could have done would have mattered—the resulting sense of powerlessness may have, one, immobilized and defeated you or, two, compelled you to seek forms of escape.

■ Jane's Story

Jane had a history of issues as a young girl, and these issues were exacerbated during her transition into adulthood. She says it began when she started hanging out with the wrong crowd. Or maybe that is just what she remembers being told by others. She does know that she started drinking at an early age, endured several abortions as the result of unprotected sex with many boys, seldom attended school as a teenager, and eventually dropped out altogether. Jane started running away as long ago as she can remember. When she was six, she wrapped up some much-loved stuffed animals into a blanket from her bed and walked away from her home. She was not upset. There was no fight. She just wanted to "go away," as she put it.

Being home felt like too much for Jane. She can't remember ever being happy to be home. She says, "I never wanted to be there. I always dreamt of leaving. I always wanted to leave. All my thoughts and dreams were about going someplace else. I didn't know where, though." For Jane, comfort was always elsewhere, wherever that might be. She knew, deep down, that it was not at home...not in the house where her mother and father lived.

Jane eventually settled down. She married and had three children. After all of the struggles growing up, it appeared that she was finally okay. Jane knew better, though. Thoughts of escape still haunted her. Yes, she loved her husband and children. She loved them, heart and soul. But she still wanted to leave. As she would drive her two eldest daughters to school in the morning, she would experience all of these thoughts about leaving and never coming back. It was like when she was a little girl. She had no idea where she would actually go. She just knew she wanted to go somewhere else, which generated tremendous conflict within her.

Jane knew it was neither good nor healthy to dream of leaving her family. She didn't really want to leave them. Yet fantasies of escape occupied her thoughts, no matter what she tried to do to be rid of them. Now Jane wanted to escape from her thoughts of wanting to escape. She wondered what spending all of those years growing up "running away" had taught her. It certainly had not taught her to stay. Then again, she never had anyone or anything in life that she wanted to stay for.

Jane's story illustrates how difficult it is to break old habits. How do you not repeat what you have always done? How do you stop running away if you are like Jane? Or, alternatively, how do you stop lying in fits of shame and guilt if you have always tried to hide the truth from others? How do you stop trying to be everything to everyone if that's always what you've done? How do you stop being the type of person you had to become in order to survive?

DOING SOMETHING DIFFERENT

You can learn to do something different. But how do you change if you're so used to the habits that you formed so young? What if you have become so accustomed to paying attention to the wishes and needs of others that you forget to pay attention to your own needs and wishes?

■ Denise's Story

Denise was your stereotypical people pleaser. She wanted to make others happy. She had a hard time saying no. In fact, it was practically impossible for her to say no. She was afraid of letting others down or disappointing them. If her boss wanted her to stay after work, that is what Denise would do. Not that this was what Denise actually wanted. She often resented having so much put on her plate. Sadly, that resentment was often dumped on her family at home. She found herself overwhelmed in the evenings when she finally came home, and this led to her snapping at her husband and two children. Asked a simple question like "Mom, do you know where my baseball glove is?" she would boil over. "How am I supposed to know where everything is? It's your glove. You find it!"

Afterward, Denise would often go into the bathroom and cry. It wasn't her children's fault. They didn't do anything wrong, and here she was snapping at them over silly little things like a missing pair of pants or a baseball glove.

Like so many who grow up with a depressed parent, Denise took on the role of caregiver early on: the one who has to do for others, to find out what everyone else needs and wants and do whatever it takes to give it to them. In many ways, Denise never had a chance to grow up and become herself. She spent a lifetime doing what everyone else around her needed to have done: staying late for her boss; volunteering in the classroom at school; watching her friends' children while her friends went out of town. As a result, she didn't know what she needed for herself. Denise was drowning while trying to live up to all of the demands and expectations being placed on her. She felt like she had no choice.

Trying to make everyone else happy and doing what they wanted was making Denise miserable. She wondered why no one else was able to see that she had enough to do, and she was furious that other people were so insensitive and kept asking her to do more and more. She would think, *Can't they see I have enough to do here already?*

For Denise, the challenge was to learn to express her own needs and wishes, which she had never learned to do while growing up. As an adult, she didn't even talk about how it felt to be burdened by all the demands being placed on her by family, friends, employers, and associates, but kept it to herself. She didn't know how to say no. In fact, she didn't even know how to say, "I'm not sure right now. Let me check my schedule and get back to you as soon as I can." In other words, Denise didn't know how to buy herself time before committing to a task.

If you recognize any part of yourself in Denise's story, you will benefit from learning how to buy yourself time rather than overcommitting yourself. You also can buy yourself a little more time before making a decision to commit your time, one way or the other. As you practice buying yourself time, you will use several important skills and behaviors discussed in this chapter—asserting yourself, telling the truth, and being present.

Exercise: Buying Yourself Time

The next time you are confronted with a situation where someone asks you to do something for them, practice buying yourself time. Please modify these statements to suit your situation, and see what happens when you begin to buy yourself time.

- "I'm really appreciative that you think so highly of me and my work that you ask me to stay late so often. I am very grateful for my job and want to do my best. However, I won't be able to continue to stay late as often as I have in the past, because I have other obligations at home."

- "I am so grateful to have you as a friend. I love coming over to your place and visiting with you and your family. Unfortunately, I can't attend this weekend. I have other plans."

- "I am so glad that I have had time to volunteer my services in the past. However, I won't be able to do as much in the future. If I have the time, I would love to. I'll call you when I'm available."

- "I'm thrilled that you're so enthusiastic about being involved in so many activities after school. It really makes me happy for you that you want to be so involved. I won't be able to take you to all of these activities, but if you pick one or two things to do after school each week, I'm confident I can make that happen for you."

- "I can't answer that question at the moment. If time frees up later today, I'd be happy to give you a call back."

These are a few examples of how you might begin to express your own needs by buying yourself time. Once you start regularly doing it, you will see the power of this simple practice.

As a child of one or more depressed parents, chances are that much of what you tend to do in your life is connected to how you tried to adapt to your parent's depressed state. As a child, you can end up developing a hypervigilant state of awareness, because you are always on guard for what your parent or parents might need from you. You want to help. You want them to be better.

What happens later in life is that you end up taking that same attitude with you into all of your relationships, be they romantic, work related, or with friends. In simple terms, the mistaken idea seems to be this: *If I just say yes, and do what is asked of me, everything will be better and maybe even fixed.*

As you may realize by now, everything does not always turn out well when you say yes to everyone and everything. For starters, you don't necessarily end up feeling or doing all that well. You can end up increasingly stressed, exhausted, worn down, and resentful. You can end up completely worn down and even physically ill due to all the commitments you have made and have to live up to. This is why buying yourself time is so important.

LIVING WITH MAYBES

Buying yourself time does not mean you are always going to say no. Sometimes a possibility is left to hang in the air for a bit while you see what transpires and how things play out. We're ultimately not in control of how everything unfolds. Things happen. Sometimes we even may need to break a commitment. That's just life. It doesn't mean we are careless with our commitments or that we frequently fail to see them through. But children get sick. Cars break down. The unexpected happens.

As a child of the depressed, you often may feel like the rest of the world is riding on your shoulders. You feel like you have to do it all. You feel like you have to make everything okay for everyone around you. It can all become a trap, a terrible, suffocating trap from which there is seemingly no escape.

■ Jennifer's Story Continued

You may recall Jennifer from chapter 4, whose depressed and alcoholic mother took out her anger on her. Jennifer's resulting hypervigilance later had a huge impact on her career choices and her relationships: "As a nurse I took care of everyone. In my social life, if anyone needed anything, I was Johnny-on-the-spot. I tried to make everyone around me okay. Whatever anyone asked of me, I found a way to say yes."

Things eventually broke down for Jennifer. At first she didn't know precisely what the problem was. Like many who first seek help, she just knew that she could not go on this way any longer. She realized that how she was acting in the world and her manner of relating to those around her was destroying her.

Over time, Jennifer realized a few more things about her behavior and how it was leaving her stressed, exhausted, bitter, and resentful. She ended up choosing a new profession, and her relationships improved. She learned how to buy herself time, by not feeling pressured to immediately say yes all the time when approached by family, friends, and coworkers. She still said yes quite often, though. She was still a good friend. Maybe even a better friend.

No one really appreciates a pushover. If you feel like a doormat, and everyone around you is using you for their own aims, then part of your responsibility is to not expect them to change. You have to stop letting others walk all over you. You have to assert your own wishes and desires. You have to tell your own truth.

You can, like Jennifer, discover that the world does not unravel if you say, "I'm not sure. I will have to check my schedule and get back to you on that." And then, when you check your schedule and see that you cannot possibly fit this one more thing into your life without something or someone suffering, you can call back and say, "I have checked my schedule, and with all the commitments that I currently have, there is just no way I can do this and do it well. I have to say no." Again, you'll see that the world will continue to turn, regardless of your response.

Remember that the right question to ask yourself is not *Can I say yes?* but rather *Is it healthy for me and my family to say yes?* The answer to that might often be no.

IT'S NOT ALL ON YOU

Maybe everything does not depend upon you. Some things do depend upon you. Maybe some people do, too. Maybe they can depend upon you a little less. Maybe they will learn to be fine with that. Maybe they won't.

There is no telling how people will respond and react to you once you start saying "no" or "maybe" or "let's wait and see." If you have always said yes and never hesitated, others around you may need to adjust. They will go through that process of adjustment—like it or not. I urge you to be deeply committed to your own health, healing, and wellness. After all, how much can someone really love you if they are willing to run you into the ground, with no concern for your well-being? Most of all, this is about you respecting yourself and caring for yourself, regardless of others' reactions.

Your family and friends will learn to appreciate that you have your own voice and that you cannot be there for them all the time. Maybe they will learn and grow with you as you heal and recover. Maybe some people in your life won't. Maybe you will discover that new friends and faces will show up who appreciate your ability to say, "Let me think about that."

And...just maybe...you will realize that in buying yourself time, you are finally learning how to be a real friend to yourself.

KEY POINTS

■ Part of the healing journey and your recovery is to challenge yourself to do things that may be uncomfortable for you at first, because you are not used to behaving in these ways.

- Be gentle with yourself as you take new steps. Remember, a bit of awkwardness is expected. So, too, is falling. Be supportive of the baby steps you are learning to take on this new path to a better life.

- Saying yes all the time can wear you down to the point that you want to run away. Learn to express your needs.

- You can buy yourself time by learning how to say "maybe" or "let me get back to you." Then you can ask yourself the right questions.

- Buying yourself time is giving yourself the gift of space, space that allows you room to breathe. Any time you feel pressured to respond is a perfect time to practice buying yourself time.

CHAPTER 7

Negotiating Your Way to Better Boundaries and Relationships

When you change your behavior to make your life better, you're not the only one who will have to make changes. All the people in your life are going to experience an adaptive period as well. If we are no longer dancing the same old steps with those close to us, then the steps they are used to using are also going to have to change. The old routines won't work anymore.

In clinical terms, focusing on the shifting dynamics of relationships as we change, grow, mature, and heal falls under the heading of *boundary work*. This chapter will help you do this work by exploring the nature of boundaries, how your own situation may have been affected by inadequate boundaries, and what you can do about it now.

DEFINING BOUNDARIES

Do you recall those times when, as a child, you drew a line in the sand and told another child, "Do not cross that line!" You were making a boundary. A boundary, in simplest terms, is what we allow others to do—or, conversely, what we do not allow others to do—when they are in relationship with us. One quick example is when someone who has suffered from domestic abuse sets a new boundary by refusing to be abused any longer. She simply will not tolerate that abuse. That is a boundary.

Even if we never consciously focus on the kinds of boundaries that we have in our relationships with others, it does not mean that we have none in place. Boundaries develop quite naturally—even automatically—over the course of our lives. Some people have healthy boundaries that allow for personal growth and development and that nurture a variety of supportive relationships. Other people experience more challenges in relationships because they lack healthy boundaries. The latter seems to be especially true for those who grew up as children of the depressed.

When We Have Unstable Boundaries

Without firm but flexible boundaries in place in our lives, your relationships with others will be marked by a number of possible difficulties. Here are some of the more common ways that unstable boundaries may look and feel in your life.

- Unstable boundaries may look like a lack of respect and feel like you are being "walked all over."

- Unstable boundaries may look like neediness and feel like you are going to die without others.

- Unstable boundaries may look like a loss of self and autonomy and feel like emptiness and deprivation.

- Unstable boundaries may look like confusion and disarray in relationships—chaos—and feel like you don't know where you end and others begin—or where you begin and others end.

It will be helpful to take a closer look at each of these common consequences of unsteady and unstable boundaries.

LACK OF RESPECT

When your boundaries with others are unstable, it can feel like others are walking all over you, and it often looks like you are not being respected. Friends and other family members may point out the problem: "I don't know why you let them do that to you. You need to stand up for yourself more. You just let everyone walk all over you."

You may nod your head in agreement when you hear this. You may know secretly in your heart that this is, at the very least, partially true. At the same time, you don't know what to do about it. In fact, you might be afraid—chillingly so—to do anything at all.

NEEDINESS

When your boundaries are unsteady and unstable, it can look like you are needy, and it can feel like you couldn't possibly survive without the presence and approval of your family and friends, even those who are walking all over you. This sense of dire need is what can prevent you from defining and renegotiating firmer and more stable boundaries with others. The fear is that if you do anything to stand up for yourself, then they will leave you and you will have nothing and no one. That's a terrifying thought.

LACK OF SELF

Unsteady and unstable boundaries can leave you feeling empty and can look to others like you have no clear sense of self and no real autonomy. Everything you do seems to depend upon others, and your entire sense of self is defined by your relationships. You may cling to others, because without them you don't know who you are. It might feel to you like you would cease to exist if you ever lost them. This is what keeps you constantly compliant and conciliatory in your relationships, whether with family, lovers, spouses, children, coworkers, or friends. Again, the fear of losing them keeps you from asserting yourself and defining your boundaries more clearly.

CHAOS

Sketchy boundaries can leave you—and your life—in a big chaotic mess. It can feel like you are doing all you can each day just to keep your head above water. It may seem to you like you are constantly putting out fires. One here. Another over there. As soon as one crisis is averted, another one shows up. Your life seems like—feels like—a never-ending set of crises, some little and some big. Always an emergency. Always some drama.

Having unstable boundaries may look different to you from chaos or the other common experiences described here. This list is by no means comprehensive. And unstable boundaries may not be your problem at all. You could have the opposite, rigid boundaries—which, while not as common for children of the depressed as unstable ones, can lead to similar dissatisfaction in your life. If you have other issues with boundaries, take a moment to reflect on them and possibly write about them in your journal. Whatever your boundary issues, as the child of a depressed parent, you can use the skills offered in this chapter to establish better boundaries in your relationships.

■ Jacob's Story

Jacob remembers when he was four and his mom went away for the summer. He never really found out why. He just remembers making weekend trips to go see her after a long drive to upstate New York. He remembers how his dad would remind him and his sister to smile when they saw Mommy. He remembers arriving and getting out of the station wagon and entering a large and somewhat imposing building. They would walk through a long corridor that ran through the center of the building, which then fed out onto a patio that overlooked the largest swath of green grass and trees he had ever seen. There, on that patio, he would sit with his dad and sister waiting for Mommy to arrive. He remembers how she looked the first time he went there to visit her that summer. Or, as he remembers it now, how she didn't look.

Jacob tried to look into his mommy's eyes. He recalls walking over to where she had been wheeled out in a wheelchair by an attendant dressed in white, and he tried to tell whether she could see him. He peered up at his mommy and saw her slumped over with no expression on her face. On the ride home, he asked, "Daddy, was Mommy sleeping with her eyes open?" His dad just kept on driving.

All Jacob remembers being told was that "Mommy is not feeling good and needs to go away, so she can rest."

Jacob's mom never did get enough rest. Even when she came home, he remembers, she needed to lie down a lot. His dad would constantly be on him and his sister about needing to keep quiet. He would say, "Don't upset your mother," and would remind them, "Don't make too much noise."

For Jacob, there was always an eerie silence about his family's home. It was quieter than any other home he remembers going to. He now compares it to a morgue. To Jacob, his mom seemed like the most fragile creature in the world. He was always anxious about what would happen to her if he did the wrong thing...if he was too loud...if he did something and he didn't know it was wrong...if he accidentally made the wrong noise at the wrong time...if he upset her.

What would happen? Would his mom die? Would he accidentally kill her if he caused any disturbance?

It is not surprising that, as an adult, Jacob still feared upsetting people. He had a hard time asserting himself. Jacob found himself unable to express what he needed or wanted in a relationship. This fear and dread of "making the wrong noise" often left him feeling quite anxious. He would do anything that someone he dated wanted him to do. This seemed to work fine, up to a point. But once the relationship started to become more serious and committed, things would quickly spiral into a chaotic brew of being "unable to end the relationship" no matter how bad things became.

Plus, he had been cheated on by virtually every girlfriend he had ever dated. This was a mystery to him, since he was the most loyal and committed man he knew. While his friends would often confess infidelity in relationships, Jacob never did, because he had none to confess. He was not the kind of person who would cheat.

Jacob felt like the "perfect guy." He was easy to get along with, keen on providing for others and their needs, and sensitive; he had a great job; he was fairly good-looking, took care of himself, and could not recall ever once starting a fight in his life. So why was he "doomed" to be approaching his forties yet unable to find someone to marry? In fact, it seemed all of his relationships followed the same pattern: he was a great guy who would do anything for the woman in his life, but whatever woman he chose would be unfaithful and in the end would dump him.

Fear of Abandonment

Fear of abandonment is a common consequence of having had a depressed parent. Like Jacob, you too may have difficulty setting good boundaries in your relationships, because you are afraid that if you express your own needs, others will reject you. In his intimate relationships, Jacob was so afraid of abandonment that he never voiced his own concerns. He avoided any issues he had and swept all his concerns under the rug. Little did he know, at the time, that this in effect invited the women in his life to push the relationship's boundaries way beyond what was healthy.

The women in Jacob's life were testing him: they wanted to know where the boundaries were in their relationship with him, and Jacob never let them know. He was afraid to. He feared that even bringing up the topic of having mixed feelings about how things were going—or expressing his own needs—would result in his being left on the spot. It was as if his old fear of upsetting his mother, somehow pushing her into a state from which she would never recover, was ruling his current actions and relationship choices. The words from his father, "Don't you upset Mommy," became the rule he lived by in his adult life: *Don't upset others. Be quiet, timid, helpful, and accommodating.* Jacob would need to learn the power of his own voice, the wisdom of his own wishes, and the truth of his own concerns.

BOUNDARIES 101

As the child of a depressed parent, you probably are going to have some personal boundary work to do. With luck, yours won't be as significant as the work Jacob discovered he had to do. It could be as simple as learning to more effectively state to others what it is about your relationship with them that does—and does not—work for you.

Exercise: What Are Your Boundary Issues?

Check all the boundary issues that apply to your life:

Unstable Boundaries

_____ You have difficulty saying no.

_____ Your needs come after others' needs.

_____ You let others push you around.

_____ You find it hard to stand up for yourself.

_____ You have a hard time stating your opinion, even when you're asked.

_____ You try to please others, even when it's not good for you.

Rigid Boundaries

_____ You always say no.

_____ Your needs are all that matters.

_____ You push other people away.

_____ You're always ready for an argument.

_____ You always say what you think, no matter whether anyone wants to know.

_____ You get angry when someone asks you to do something.

You may want to write in the space provided or your journal about any others boundary issues that you may have. Many children of the depressed have boundaries that are either too rigid or too unstable. What is your tendency?

_____

_____

If you tend to have flimsy and unstable boundaries, then the primary work for you is going to be in learning how to be firm, as Jacob discovered. On the other hand, if your boundaries are too rigid and inflexible, then the primary work for you is going to be relaxing your boundaries somewhat and discovering how to be more flexible. Either way, the healthy goal remains the same: to have firm but flexible boundaries that clearly outline the healthy codes of conduct you expect in your relationships with others.

So, how do you establish and maintain better boundaries? Here are some basic steps:

1. Define good boundaries.

2. Protect those boundaries.

3. Respond to boundary offenders.

Here's a closer look at how to establish and maintain better boundaries.

Define Good Boundaries

As you learned earlier in this chapter, boundaries are really nothing more than a set of guidelines by which we negotiate our way through relationships. People with unsteady boundaries might find that others are constantly trespassing those boundaries in one way or another. People with very rigid boundaries might find that no one wants to be around them, because they are too tight and controlling in how they negotiate their relationships. The goal is having boundaries like a tree's branches, firmly rooted but with the flexibility to adapt to changing winds.

The goal, then, is to acquire and maintain firm but flexible boundaries as you engage in relationships with others. Planting firm but flexible boundaries means that you occasionally accommodate others, due to the often unpredictable nature of life, but you also maintain your self-respect and dignity by not allowing others to take advantage of you. Likewise, this means that you expect others to accommodate you on occasion, but you know that they can't be at your beck and call.

Protect Your Boundaries

Once you define good boundaries, it's your job to protect them. Imagine that your life is a garden where you can grow fruits and vegetables to feed yourself and your family, and gorgeous flowers that adorn the landscape with outpourings of beauty and fragrance. Now imagine doing all of the work it takes to grow what nourishes you: all of the loving effort put into selecting the right plants and deciding where to plant them, in turning the soil, and in lovingly watering these plants and flowers that feed and sustain you on so many levels.

Now, imagine someone coming in and trampling on everything you have put into your garden, someone who does not care at all about this garden that you find so uplifting and inspiring. This is why it's important to have boundaries—to protect that which you have worked for and value.

Similarly, to nurture ourselves, we need to have protective personal boundaries that clearly define and express to others that "Only care and respect are welcome here!" If we don't have these personal boundaries, then we are vulnerable to the reckless disregard of others.

Likewise, we don't want to be so rigid that we never allow others to enter. Finding the right balance is important.

Maintaining the firmness and flexibility of your personal boundaries is one of the more essential tasks that you can undertake in your healing journey. The goal is to take responsibility for requiring respect from others—not asking permission for it, but requiring it.

Respond to Boundary Offenders

Typically, others around us who disregard our boundaries do so because they don't recognize or know our boundaries, which falls under the heading of *ignorant disregard*. They don't know what matters to us. They don't know how important our healing journey is. They don't know how deeply and desperately we may need this healing and how crucial it is to our well-being. They simply are unaware that these precious little flowers in our garden are so meaningful to us.

When others don't know, you need to communicate what your boundaries are. If others show ignorant disregard for your boundaries, it is up to you to calmly, but clearly, speak up and say what your boundaries are. If they forget, you will need to remind them.

You can practice with these statements (or modify them to suit your needs):

- "I understand that you didn't know this before, since I never mentioned it. Please call first to ask if it's a good time, before coming over. Thanks for understanding."

- "As I said before, I cannot help you on Sundays. I'll be over on Monday, as planned."

- "I'm done with being called names. When you can speak to me respectfully, give me a call."

More often than not, those around you will gladly heed your gentle but firm reminder to be more careful. If not, then they fall into a second camp of boundary offenders who will show *inconsiderate disregard* for what you need. This is where reminding others of our personal boundaries doesn't have much effect. These are the people who just don't care. As a result, more extreme measures are required.

So what can you do? In truly extreme cases—like those in which domestic abuse is a factor—there is often no recourse outside of engaging the courts and pursuing a restraining order. In most situations, if we have people in our lives who disregard our needs and our voice—people to whom our saying no means nothing, people who want to relegate us to being someone who serves their whims and desires—then we have no alternative besides removing ourselves from their sphere of influence. Either we do what we can to make sure they are not welcome in our space or we do what we can to limit our time in their space.

In most cases, however, the people in our lives who transgress our boundaries do so out of ignorance or old habit. When you finally tell them what you need, they will want to make adjustments to accommodate you, even if you never imagined they could.

■ Susie's Story

As far back as Susie can remember, her mother was standing over her. Susie can't remember a time when she did not feel her mother's eyes digging into the back of her head. Even as a child, she recalls feeling like someone was always looking over her shoulder. In school, she would often turn around suddenly to see if someone was there. No one would be there, of course, but she had to look. That is how powerful her mother's impact was on her.

Now that she is older, Susie knows why her mother was this way. Her mom grew up the oldest child of a poor rural family in Missouri. As a result, she had to grow up way too fast. She had younger siblings to look after all the time. She was always responsible. She had to be. She developed depression as a teenager and never sought help. Marrying an alcoholic at a young age and then having children right away meant that Susie's mother always had to take care of everything. It never stopped for her. Now she had her own children to watch over as well as her alcoholic husband, who never helped around the house and who would begin drinking as soon as he came home from work.

As an adult, Susie loathed those times when her mother would invite herself to come and stay for a week or two in the summer, and the end-of-the-year holidays were even worse. To Susie, it seemed as if she could not be far enough away from her mother. It was so hard for Susie to be around her, even with knowledge of her past and how it had shaped her. Why couldn't she just talk with her mom like a normal person? Why did she not want to return her mom's phone calls? Why were the holidays terrible instead of a joyous occasion for celebration and renewal? Why was it so hard for her to have a relationship with her mom? Why couldn't her mom just relax and let her be, for once? Just for once! Was it too much to ask?

Like Susie, you may come to understand why your depressed parent had the problems that he or she had, and you may come to understand the impact of these problems on you. But as you already know, information by itself is typically not enough to change the quality of our lives. You have to act on that information if you want to effect any change. For Susie, knowing why her mother behaved as she did was not enough. Since her mother had trouble recognizing Susie's boundaries, it was Susie's job to tell her what they were.

SKILL BUILDER: ASSERTIVE ACCEPTANCE

When working with our boundaries and renegotiating the terms of significant relationships as we heal our childhood wounds, we need to practice the skill of *assertive acceptance*. This does not mean saying, "Oh well, I guess I will just have to live with things being like this...there is nothing I can do about it." It means that we can establish firm but flexible boundaries only by first accepting that we cannot wait for others to change. When we accept others as they are—and stop expecting them to change or even hoping that they'll change—we can begin to assert ourselves in our relationships. For example, Susie wanted her mother to change, to begin to appreciate Susie for who she was, and not always dominate her as if she were still a little child. But Susie also recognized that her mom was not simply going to wake up one day being more sensitive and more thoughtful and considerate to Susie—as Susie had wished for years. For their relationship to change, Susie had to finally accept her mother's ways and then assert her own needs and wishes.

We can't make others change, even if their changing in certain ways would help both them and us. Instead, we have to concentrate on developing sufficient life skills and not hold out the hope that others around us will change, develop, and grow. Maybe they will. Maybe they won't. Ultimately, what others decide to do is not in our hands. What is in our hands is how we choose to define the boundaries of our relationships with them. What Susie ended up doing when her mother invited herself to visit can serve as a good example of how to practice assertive acceptance.

◼ Susie's Story Continued

When her mother announced how she had already purchased a plane ticket and was coming out to stay for a week to help with the kids (never mind that Susie hinted to her mother a few times that she didn't want her help), Susie felt her heart begin to race. Her stomach was turning inside out. She had never been able to state clearly what she wanted or needed from her mother.

This would be the first time Susie had ever openly expressed her needs to her mom about what felt right for Susie. She began haltingly. "Mom, we all really love you and want you to come and stay, but it is hard for me when you visit. When we spend lots of time together, you begin criticizing every move I make, and I just don't want to hear that anymore. I know you mean well, but my life is already stressful enough with work and the kids. Too much time together is hard for all of us, including you, since the house becomes really tense. So, if you come, it would work best if you stay in a hotel in town. We could all meet for dinner, or you could come and stay here at the house with the kids during the day while I'm at work. I know they love seeing you."

This speech was followed by an eerie silence on the other end of the line. Then Susie heard her mom crying, which almost undid Susie. She thought to herself, *I should just let her come and stay here. It's not that bad.*

Something deep inside her, however, would not let those words come out. Instead, she asked, "Mom, are you okay?"

Her mom answered with a crack in her voice, "No. I am not okay. Who wants to be rejected by their own daughter?"

Susie took a deep breath. "I am not rejecting you. I just need things to be different between us, and getting some space while you visit is a good way to begin a new and better relationship."

"I am just trying to help you, Susie," her mom said. "I had no idea you felt this way. Why didn't you tell me this before?"

"I never could," replied Susie. "I didn't think you would listen. And I didn't want to hurt your feelings. You are my mom. I love you. It doesn't make me feel good to say that I don't want you to come and stay at my house, but I want things to be better between us, and I think it's a good idea."

"Have you always felt like this?" her mom asked.

"Yes, for a long time I have," Susie said. "I know, as I was growing up, it was hard for you with Dad and us kids. I know why you had to be in charge all the time. But things are different now, Mom. I'm not a kid anymore, and Dad has been gone for nearly fifteen years. You can't treat me like I'm eleven and expect everything to be okay between us. It isn't."

Susie's mother had never heard such words from her daughter before. How could she have known how Susie felt if Susie never expressed her authentic feelings to her?

Susie's mom was left with a choice. Would she disown her daughter because she was so upset by her daughter's assertiveness? Would she withdraw and become depressed and reticent? Would she lose her cool and blow up at Susie and call her all sorts of names? Or would she feel her own daughter's truth being spoken to her and then take that truth to heart, thereby offering them both an opportunity to evolve and grow their mother-daughter bond in new ways?

I'm happy to report that although it took a few more negotiations before her trip, Susie's mom adapted to the new arrangement, and now the two of them are both working hard on creating a healthier relationship.

The irony is that when Susie finally accepted that her mother was not going to change and then asserted her own needs in their relationship, her mother actually did change. It was worth it to Susie to speak truthfully to her mother, since she had hope that her mother would eventually hear her. She was, however, prepared to distance herself more if her mother wasn't capable of working on the relationship. With some people in your life, you might not think it worthwhile to expend the energy that Susie did. You can learn to accept them for who they are and then decide what kind of relationship, if any, you wish to have.

Exercise: Practicing Assertive Acceptance

Think of someone in your life with whom you could practice the skill of assertive acceptance. For example, do you have someone in your life who annoys or frustrates you? If you have a relationship with somebody yet often dread the thought of spending time with that person, then this relationship would be a good choice for this exercise. Now follow these steps:

1. Acknowledge to yourself that this person will not suddenly change or approach you differently just because you wish it. You already know this rationally, but emotionally you probably keep hoping this person will change and hence feel frustrated when this doesn't happen. Say to yourself, *I want this person to change without me having to say anything, but that's a fantasy.*

2. Imagine what you might say to this person to help your relationship. What does this person need to know about you? For instance, does he need to know that the language he uses grates on your nerves? Or does she need to know that you don't want to get together every day after work and you would rather meet once a week? Practice stating firmly but kindly to this person what you'd prefer. For example you might practice saying, "Sometimes the words you choose sound harsh to me. Can you try and curb it a bit?" Or "I've been ignoring some of my responsibilities after work. It would work better for me if we meet one day a week. Is Wednesday or Thursday better for you?"

3. Now imagine what kind of response you might receive. (Hopefully, you'll get a positive, respectful one, and often you will.) Practice in your mind staying calm but firm about what you require, regardless of the response. You can also suggest talking more about it later if the person isn't receptive to what you're saying.

Now go ahead and say what you need to say to this person in your life. You will probably be happy that you did, and you might wonder why you waited so long. It's okay—you weren't ready before.

Occasionally, when someone sets new boundaries, it results in the end of the relationship. This, however, is not the norm. You will need to be prepared for the possibility that when you practice the skill of assertive acceptance, there will be those who will not know how to deal with the new you. It will upset the status quo, and your relationship will effectively have nothing to stand upon, at least temporarily. What loss is that, though, if the relationship has been built upon a foundation of unsteady and unstable boundaries? What loss is it if the relationship is unhealthy and has been so for a long time?

NEW BEGINNINGS

More often than not, when we renegotiate our relationships—by establishing new boundaries that are both firm and flexible—we create new beginnings. Stating what we need and want in our relationships—creating healthy boundaries in our lives with others—seems to open up pathways of communication that are open, honest, and authentic for everyone involved.

More often than not, those around us are surprised to hear how we feel and to find out what we need. This is true, mostly, because we have probably not previously shared any of this with them in such an assertive way. We are more likely to hear "I had no idea you felt that way" than "How dare you say such a thing to me!"

Even if you have some anxiety about erecting appropriate new boundaries—and may have some rocky stretches to navigate as you practice these new skills—don't let this stop you from taking action. In fact, you might discover that many of your closest relationships are given a fresh start as you establish new boundaries that redefine the nature of your connection.

KEY POINTS

- As you heal and recover from your early wounds of being a child of the depressed, odds are you will need to renegotiate the boundaries of many of your close relationships.

- Personal boundaries that are either too unsteady and unstable or too strict and firm may be your inheritance as a child of the depressed.

- The goal in boundary work is to erect and maintain firm but flexible boundaries that are like tree branches—deeply rooted, yet able to bend with the winds of change, time, and situation.

- Assertive acceptance means learning to accept the reality that some of the people who disregard your boundaries will not change on their own, and that they might never change, so it is up to you to define the boundaries of your relationship with them.

- Most of your relationships will be given a fresh start and a new beginning, as stating your own needs and desires in an assertive way will give others a firm place from which they can to relate to you.

CHAPTER 8

The Patient Path to Wellness

You have come a long way on your journey to healing. You have learned much about how your life up until now has been affected by having a depressed parent. You have explored the impact on your own thoughts and actions, and begun to make some important changes based on this information. Encountering so much new material can be both exciting and a bit overwhelming. Moreover, while learning about what you can do to improve your life can be a good deal of work in itself, actually incorporating what you've learned into your life can be the greater challenge. You may ask yourself any of these questions:

- *Why am I not feeling better immediately?*

- *Why is this taking so long?*

- *Why am I not past all of this already?*

- *When am I going to feel normal?*

- *How much of this work do I have to do?*

- *What if I never get better?*

- *What if I'm doomed? Cursed? Inherently defective?*

- *Who is ever going to want to really love someone like me?*

Having such worries and considerations is par for the course. It comes with the territory. Furthermore, you are not crazy if some days you feel like you won't ever get better. You are not incurable and doomed if there are moments when you snap at someone you love. It is not the end of the world if you slip up from time to time. This chapter will help you look at how you are approaching this journey and offer some helpful tools, such as exercising patience, avoiding comparisons with others, and accepting yourself for who you are. It will offer the stories of several adult children of the depressed, so you can see how others have coped with difficulties along the way.

■ Steve's Story

The first time we met, I could see that Steve wanted all of this to be over with, probably even before he walked through my door! He fidgeted in his seat constantly. He seemed to look at his watch nearly every other minute. It was obvious from his body language and posture that he wanted to get up and out of that seat—or better yet, run right out of the room—so I asked him if he wanted to leave. He seemed shocked at first. For the first time, he actually looked me in the eye. He was checking to see if I was serious or not. I was.

Steve informed me that he was there only because he had to be. His wife was making him go to a therapist. He said, matter-of-factly, "I don't have time for this."

Steve's case was perhaps the extreme. If your goal is to get it over with before you've even begun, you won't make much progress. But then, does anyone really ever want to take time out of their day to heal, to recover, and to become whole again? Does an athlete who tears up a knee in competition really want to go and have surgery, and then be told that she has a year or more of therapy before she'll be able to continue with her favorite sport? Do any of us really have time for this business of healing?

Doesn't each and every one of us want our injury to be gone as soon as possible so that we're back at full strength as quickly as possible? It's probably safe to say that we all want to be well and whole again but don't necessarily want to go through what it takes to be well and whole again.

The point is that we need to make the time to allow ourselves to properly heal. We have to work on exercising patience.

HAVE PATIENCE

Patience doesn't necessarily come easily when we are in recovery from old wounds that never truly healed before. It's like having a broken bone that was set improperly the first time, so now that same bone must be rebroken and set again in a way that will allow for proper healing. Going through such a painful process—even if the eventual outcome is worth it—is not easy for any of us.

It would be easier if you could just go on with your life and not have to worry about all of this healing business, wouldn't it? But wasn't just going on with your life the problem to begin with? Remember, you dove into the realm of your own healing because you needed to do it. You need to keep in mind that the way things were wasn't very good for you and probably wasn't very good for those around you, either.

■ Theresa's Story

Theresa has been a client over the past twenty years, off and on. I typically see her for a couple of months, we do some good work together, and then she stops coming. A couple of years later, I will hear from her again, and then we will do the same thing: she comes to see me once a week for a couple of months, and then she just stops. This has been going on for roughly two decades, with six or seven cycles of starting and stopping. Importantly, Theresa's process works for her. She feels that she is improving, but she chooses to work in spurts, as she takes her time integrating her new life skills and practices. Then, when she is ready, she comes back for more.

I often have the impression that Theresa thinks the healing process should be easier or that she wishes it would be easier. She would like it to go faster, but at the same time she knows how she needs to do this work and wisely respects her own process.

Healing does go faster for some people than it does for others, and there is really no way to tell in advance. No one knows how any of us is going to respond to this kind of healing and recovery work. I have had people come through my door who, I assumed at the beginning, would not come to see me for very long; but instead they end up deeply invested in their own healing and recovery for an extended period of time. There are others who, before I know it, are done with this work: much happier, much healthier, and ready to continue moving forward with their lives.

It's important to adapt your expectations to your own situation rather than have any set expectations about how long the healing process will take. As an analogy, the common cold usually lasts four to seven days, but for some people it will linger for weeks, while others have sniffles for only a couple of days. Who is to say why? It is pretty much the same way with psychological healing. You just never know.

AVOID COMPARISONS

Being the social creatures we are, it is next to impossible to avoid comparing ourselves to others from time to time. Comparison comes naturally. We do it as a result of our being socialized by living in groups. Whether it is family, a tribe of close friends, our coworkers, or a religious organization, we each are embedded in one or more social groups. As a result of that, we cannot help but compare ourselves to those around us.

In certain contexts, of course, comparison can serve a valuable purpose. For instance, did you ever compare notes with your friends or classmates in college or high school to see if you were missing anything? I am sure you did. That sort of comparison can be helpful. It can help us help one another by filling in any blanks we may have missed.

In other contexts, though, comparison is not the right tool for the job. In fact, comparison can be like using a blunt object like a hammer for a situation that requires surgical precision. This is especially true in the case of psychological healing. Be kind to yourself, and avoid comparing your life, health, and happiness with anyone else's. This is the time to focus on your own life, your own health, your own healing process.

■ Katherine's Story

Katherine was quite the social butterfly, as she would freely admit with some amusement. In our few sessions, I had to regularly help her focus on herself and her own process. She seemed more interested in talking about her friends, and wondering about how she did or did not measure up to them, than she was in investing in her own work. She would say, "My neighbor bought the most expensive carpet she could find, and she couldn't afford it—isn't that irresponsible?" Or she would say, "Marcia has twice as many clothes as I do—it's not fair at all." Katherine was so externally motivated that it was difficult for her to talk about herself.

Even Katherine's own healing potential was being clubbed by her incessant focus on what everyone else was doing and experiencing. She would say, "My friend said that when she did that, she cried nonstop for a week!" Or she would say, "Well, I talked with my husband about that, and he said that he thought it was a little goofy to keep track of my thoughts. He couldn't see the point in it." When I'd ask her again, very directly, about what *she* thought or felt, she refused to really consider it.

It's important to focus on your own thoughts and feelings and behaviors, what you are doing or not doing, and avoid concentrating on what others are doing or not doing. That is the only way you will heal. Katherine ended her few therapy sessions before I had time to truly find out what she thought and felt about so many of the important things in her life. More importantly, she stopped before *she* had time to truly find out what she thought and felt about so many of these important things.

ACCEPT YOURSELF

Wouldn't it be easy if we just blossomed the way we blossomed, like plants, without giving any thought or generating any resistance based on whether we were blossoming on schedule or in the right way compared to others?

But what if it *were* that easy? What if you are flowering (or floundering, if you happen to feel like that today) as perfectly as only you can? What if you don't need to compare yourself to other people and your journey to what theirs have been? What if you don't need to have expectations about how long it will take you to heal? What if you can just be where you are now, doing what you are doing, being how you are being, and be okay with that? The truth is, you can.

You can be how you are without needing to explain it, defend it, rationalize it, justify it, protect it, or curse who you are and how you became that way. After all, you don't have to make an effort for the sun to rise—it just does. And you don't try to grow—you just grow.

There is no yardstick that you need to measure yourself against when it comes to your healing and recovery. You don't need to explain to your mother why you are not like your sister. You don't need to justify to your spouse why you are passionate about what you are passionate about. You don't need to defend yourself against all of those inherited thoughts about how you don't measure up. Remember, those thoughts are lies that keep digging under your skin and reopening old wounds, keeping them fresh in your awareness.

Each time that you hear one of those lies in your head— meaning, each time you feel compelled to compare yourself to some arbitrary measuring stick—use the SCARS technique explored in chapter 4: Stop, Congratulate, Apologize, Replace, and Smile.

GIVE YOURSELF TIME

Time—and hard work to explore and change your automatic and inherited thoughts—will eventually heal these wounds. But this probably won't happen right away. While instantaneous healing and recovery is something you may wish for, the more trustworthy aim is to be mindful that time is on your side.

Exercise: Visualizing Your Progress

Imagine you are a plant in a garden. It could be any plant, like a tomato plant or perhaps a strawberry one. So this tender little plant that is you is eagerly growing (and without effort; remember, you just grow). You have pierced the soil and are rising up toward the sky. You feel the rain gently fall upon you and nourish your roots that hold you firm to the earth. You feel the sun and moon above shining down upon you. You are a happy plant. You have your whole life ahead of you.

Unfortunately, stuff happens in life. Stuff even happens to tomato plants and strawberry plants. Winds come. Varmints invade. Pests propagate. You are attacked and your existence is threatened. You have to put all of your reserves into preserving your being. You harness all the power you have to hold together under this duress. You may even begin to wonder if you will ever fulfill your destiny and bear fruit someday. Will anyone ever be able to enjoy you? Will anyone ever get to know how delicious you are? You feel like you might not make it.

Fortunately, some unexpected blessings come to you. Someone comes and props you up after the winds cease. Someone else erects boundaries to protect you from the invading varmints. And another person removes the pests from your stalk and stems. You have a chance now. Although you have always kept growing physically, now you're not conserving all of your energy, dedicating it to merely surviving and holding on without budding or blooming. Now you can use some of that energy for new growth and blossoms. Now you can bear fruit. Now you can continue to live knowing that someone will one day enjoy you. Now you can greet the sun shining down upon you with the realization that your being and existence will nourish others. Now you know why you have come to exist and still do.

It's important to remember that our healing journey is a process. It does not happen all at once. You could say that it is never really done and over with. Many of the skills needed to heal and recover from your past are the exact same skills that make for a more joyous and wholesome life. It does not mean that rains will not come or that winds will not blow. It just means that you now have the skills and the support you need to better handle whatever comes your way. You learn how to support yourself. You learn how to ask for support from others. You also learn how to remove yourself from the influence of those who are nonsupportive.

The impact of these skills cannot be overstated. These are life skills that remain effective for the long term. You can use these tools as often as you need them. You may use them so often that they start to become a fundamental part of who you are.

What You Can Expect

Learning and applying new skills can be pretty awkward at first. Much of what this book offers certainly does not come naturally. If it did, then you would already be doing it, right? There is always a bit of a learning curve. You simply cannot rush the healing process or the learning process. If you do, the risk is that you will not heal properly and have full function restored.

Growing up, I knew a boy who broke his leg in numerous places and ended up in a full leg cast. The issue with him was that he would just not stop, and he would not use crutches. He kept going and going. It didn't seem like his parents could slow him down, either. Although his spirit was admirable, he needed to put some of that spirit into healing.

As a result, his leg never healed properly. He walked with a limp all throughout school and for the rest of his life.

My old schoolmate didn't give the healing process—and his body—the downtime that was required when he was a child. Maybe he wasn't able to. His story serves to illustrate that it simply takes time to heal.

You cannot rush the process you are in as you are healing. It takes however long it takes.

What If You Never Heal?

In the movie *As Good As It Gets*, Jack Nicholson's character is shown leaving his therapist's office. He exits through the waiting room where five or six other people are waiting for their turn to see the therapist. He stops and looks at them patiently reading their magazines and says, "What if this is as good as it gets?"

What if this is as good as it gets? What if you never feel like you are going to be better? What if the sense that something is amiss doesn't leave you? You may ask yourself, "What if I'm not going to get better?" This is what Janice did.

■ Janice's Story

Janice had been in and out of therapy for nearly a decade before she came to me. She was a very attractive young woman in her mid-thirties who had never been married and who found relationships difficult at best and impossible at worst. She struggled with her career. She had a master's degree in art history but worked as a barista in a local café.

In our first meeting together, she said that she just wanted to get better so that she could "finally get on with my life." Janice told me how her mother was supported her whole life by her father—both emotionally and financially. Her mother had received a master's in English literature before getting married and was going to teach, but then after having her first child, Janice's brother, she fell into depression. Janice was born a couple of years later.

Her mother was treated for depression, but Janice said that over time, her mother grew worse and worse. She became totally disabled during Janice's teenage years. When Janice finally went off to college, she was relieved to be out of the home, but would fight anxious feelings that she was, in her words, "slowly becoming just like my mom." That, she said, is when she started into her own downward spiral.

"As long as I had something to do to keep my mind busy—a paper to write, a test to study for—I was okay. It was like being busy was my way of waging this war against my thoughts. Having something to do kept me from becoming like Mom. I didn't want to stop. I hated silence. I didn't even want to sleep. I did everything I could to stay in motion all the time. That is why when I received my college degree, I immediately enrolled in grad school. I had to do something. I had to keep going."

After grad school, Janice went to Europe to intern at an art museum in Denmark. At first it was wonderful. She was busy as ever. The distance from home seemed to be helping her. She felt like she might finally be okay, after all. Maybe this was her redemption from all the real and imagined struggles she had gone through, which essentially boiled down to her having had no mother for much of her life. "Maybe," Janice thought to herself, "I won't become like my mom."

Janice fell in love with a Danish man several years her senior. Life was good. Really good. But then, it all suddenly fell apart. Janice's mother passed away while

Janice was in Denmark, and Janice had to come home. She said, "I am not sure what happened. I don't know if it was leaving my lover and having to take that trip back home all alone, or if it was my mother's passing, or if it was everything together, that broke me down. I have never felt the same since."

After her mother's death, guilt set in. She hated her mom for ruining her first chance at a "good life," and then felt guilty for hating her. "After my mom died, I was torn. My dad didn't have anybody, and I didn't realize how taking care of my mom all of those years had become so important to him. He would tell me, 'I don't know what I am going to do without your mother,' and I would feel guilty. I decided not to go back to Europe. I moved in with my father. It was only supposed to be for six months or so. He just needed some time to adjust, and then I would go back to Europe to finish my internship."

That never happened for Janice. She moved in with her dad so he would not have to be alone, and ended up staying with him for nearly two years before finally moving into an apartment nearby. Her life has been on hold ever since.

Twelve years later, she said, "I don't know what happened. I know I should have never moved in with Dad. I should have gone back to Europe right after my mother's funeral. I put my life on hold. I can remember phone calls with my boyfriend in Denmark—how he was growing impatient, and how I would put him off. I would tell him that I needed a little more time. Now it seems like the story of my life. Just a little more time and I will be okay. Just a little more time and I can complete my internship. Just a little more time and I will be happy. Just a little more time and I can finally get on with my own life again and not be tied up so much with my dad and worrying about him, or my mom and resenting her and her depression. Just a little more time."

Janice's healing—or what she felt and believed her healing would look and feel like to her—was preventing anything from really taking off, or taking root, in her life. It was as if she were waiting to feel okay first, and only then would she give herself permission to really start living her life. Janice's story illustrates that you can't put your life on hold while you wait for healing to begin. Remember that part of healing is taking actions that will improve your life.

GETTING IT JUST RIGHT

This chapter began with a story about Steve, which highlighted the importance of patience on your healing journey. Steve was ready to leave and get on with life before he'd ever really begun the sort of healing process he clearly needed. Steve didn't have enough time. There was never enough time. He was leaving and on his way out before he'd even arrived.

At the other extreme, Janice thought she needed more time to complete her healing before she could get her life going again. She was never okay enough to begin living her life again. After her mother passed, she found it impossible to move on. Even after more than a decade, Janice was still feeling stuck.

Neither Steve nor Janice was wrong—they each did what they needed to do—but their stories highlight the unique and contrasting reactions that are possible when moving forward with this kind of work. Together these two stories represent two extremes that we may face as we attempt to heal: rush through everything and never really heal properly, because we don't take the time to do so; or become stuck in place, so that we cannot move forward, because we believe we need more time to heal.

So what does this mean for you and your journey? How do you get it right? On the one hand, you need to give yourself time to heal. On the other you hand, you can't let this process get in the way of your life.

You probably remember the story of Goldilocks, who found one bowl of porridge too hot and another too cold, but then found a bowl of porridge that was just right for her. You want to find a healing trajectory that is just right for you. That may mean that you need a little more time or a little less. Rather then move too slow or too fast, you need to find the pace that suits you best, so that you can fully recover and heal.

Consider the possibility that you can get your healing process just right. You can find the right pace. There is a perfect path and process that is yours and yours alone.

KEY POINTS

- It is highly likely that you will become impatient with the pace of your healing process at some point. This is natural and no cause for alarm, but the idea that you are behind where you should be is just not true.

- Expectations about how fast or quickly you will move forward on your healing journey are self-defeating and counterproductive.

- Comparisons to others and how their journey has unfolded need to be taken very lightly, if at all. There simply is no one-size-fits-all approach when it comes to healing.

- There can be some awkwardness as you learn new steps, skills, and routines. With enough practice and patience, though, these new approaches can become second nature.

- Be wary of putting off your life because you believe you need to heal yourself completely first. You can still live your life and find enjoyment in the day-to-day realities of living as you are healing.

- Seek the path and pace of recovery that is neither too fast nor too slow but feels just right to you.

CHAPTER 9

Stepping Back to Have
Peace in the Present

Much of this book has focused on helping you make better sense of your own past as the child of a depressed parent. Having a general understanding of your depressed parent's condition—as well as the impact it had upon you—can ease the burden of your ceaseless wondering. You don't have to guess why anymore. You don't have to blame yourself. Instead of feeling the crushing weight of *why* all the time, now you know. Shedding a lot of light on a very dark and mysterious situation can help you learn, grow, and adapt. It allows you to move forward with understanding and perhaps a little more love and wisdom in your heart.

Hopefully by now you have a much better sense of what happened to you as a child. You have been able to put together many of the pieces of your past. You may feel that you have more work to do. I encourage you to do this work. Gaining a better understanding of why things occurred the way they did will help you form a path forward. It will allow you to live more freely in the present.

This chapter will introduce the positive practice of taking a step back to gain greater insight in the present. This practice can be used whenever you need to gain some perspective to know how to move forward.

◾ Sheryl's Story

Sheryl was sent off to boarding school at a very young age. She was only eight. Her father was in the military, and her mom didn't want to be bothered with a child around the house. As Sheryl put it, "She couldn't manage having someone around to tend to while she was alone. My dad was gone for months at a time. First she enrolled my brother in boarding school, then me. At the time, I was relieved. I say that because I can recall how down my mom's energy was. Even as a child, I felt like she was overwhelmed by the slightest little thing. Even normal stuff—everyday stuff that all parents should know how to do—was too much for her. I thought going away to boarding school was my ticket to an amazing life. I imagined it would be wonderful, and I would have all of these friends. Little did I know what was in store."

Sheryl ended up spending virtually her whole childhood in boarding schools. "We would come home for the holidays and a couple of weeks in the summer. When my dad was home, my folks would come and see my brother and me at the school where we lived. The truth is, I rarely was around my mom and dad. To this day, they are virtually strangers to me. I mean, I know them, but I don't really know them."

Sheryl struggled as a young woman. She spoke at length about how her mom didn't want to be bothered with her. Her mom made Sheryl feel like she was putting her out whenever Sheryl would ask a question or needed something. "Eventually, I stopped communicating with her in any real way," Sheryl said. "And I tried to never need anything from her. Instead, I always found a way on my own."

Throughout her twenties and thirties, Sheryl stayed as far away from her mom and dad as possible. She would make excuses as to why she could not attend family holidays. She even lived overseas for some time. Eventually, though, she made her way back home; that is, she found herself. She realized that she had been running away: "I was avoiding my mother. I was doing what she did to me! I wasn't any different. I was giving her what her disease wanted. I can remember being stuck in Thailand, not knowing anyone, nearly broke, and I thought to myself, *What on earth are you doing? You are letting your mother control you. You aren't doing this because your childhood was healthy and well adjusted. You are doing this because it wasn't healthy. So how can this be healthy now?*"

That was the moment that Sheryl pieced together her past. It had taken many years and a lot of wandering. But something eventually clicked. Sheryl realized that how she was acting was a direct result of how her mother had behaved toward her as a child. In this way, Sheryl had been not acting freely. Sure, she might have been traveling the world, but her reasons for doing so were a direct result of a condition her mother was afflicted with when Sheryl was young.

Sheryl stopped avoiding her past and stopped running from her mother and father. "I decided that it was time to face my past, to confront my own upbringing, and find a way to make it all work, even if I didn't know how to do that or what that way would be."

If we have not pieced together the past enough to resolve it in our own minds, then it becomes this haunting burden that we cannot escape. At the same time, when we do eventually piece together the past, what we've been going through makes more sense, the past becomes less of a haunting burden, and our way forward becomes all the more clear.

GAINING PERSPECTIVE

Sometimes we need to take a step back in order to see things more clearly. The truth is that as much as we believe a close-up view will be the more authentic, real, and detailed one, we can also lose perspective when we are too close to something or someone. This is what happened with Sheryl. It was not until she gained enough perspective—literally running away—that she was able to see herself, her mother, and her upbringing in a new way.

There are times when we all need to step back. It might be for just a moment, buying yourself a little time (see chapter 6), or it might take some years, as in Sheryl's case, before you have the perspective that you need to move forward in your life.

Sometimes if you are feeling under some sort of pressure, you may need to take a step back from a specific situation. The pressure may be coming from within you or from outside sources. Either way, when you feel pressured, it's better to get some distance on the situation rather than simply to react.

You may need to take a step back emotionally. Getting perspective is not always about physical distance, though sometimes stepping back physically can be helpful, as it was in Sheryl's case. Stepping back can also be helpful when you've become too invested in a certain outcome, such as being emotionally tied to things turning out a certain way. Maybe, as in Susie's case (see chapter 7), you will find yourself emotionally invested in an outcome that requires someone else to change.

As you discovered through Susie's story—and the lesson on assertive acceptance—being tied to a certain outcome prevents any real healing from taking place. It is when we lose our attachment to outcome and open up to whatever might happen that we allow an opening for something truly new and potentially redeeming to come to the fore.

GAINING CLARITY

Taking a step back can be hard, though. We are so used to the notion that we need to dig in, that we need to try harder, and that we need to really work something through before change can take place. Sometimes this is the case: we really do need to dive in deeper and delve into areas where, through our concerted effort, we can effect change. Other times, being so close hinders us. We don't have perspective. We are tied too much to our own notions of a preferable outcome. We are not letting the whole situation breathe.

Maybe you have heard how you can ruin a good meal by messing with the food too much. There's no need to flip a steak on the grill ten times. You don't need to stir that pot of soup every five minutes. When we do too much and try too hard—and what is really needed is some distance, space, and perspective—we risk turning a situation into a bigger and bigger mess.

It may be counterintuitive to suggest that doing less will accomplish more, but this is often the case. Imagine yourself with a jar of water that also has some dirt in it. Now, if you keep shaking up that jar, the water will never become clear. It will stay cloudy. But what if you allow that jar to sit? What if you leave it alone for a while? What do you think will happen to the water then? Won't the water clear up?

What if the same is possible for us in some situations? What if things become cloudy and confused because there are times when we are not letting things settle? What if stepping back, buying ourselves some time, and leaving a troublesome situation alone for a while is what we need to do to gain some clarity?

PRACTICING STEPPING BACK

There are times when life seems to conspire to grant us the distance we need. Other times we consciously choose to step back. For example, Sheryl thought she was making a conscious choice to put distance between herself and her upbringing. In hindsight, and with the perspective granted by time and distance, Sheryl realized that leaving was a way of reacting to her upbringing. She was avoiding her mom and dad just as her mom had avoided Sheryl when she was a child. It may have looked different to everyone else. It may have seemed that Sheryl was miles away and free from the impact of her childhood. Sheryl, in a moment of bracing self-honesty, knew better. She was carrying her mother with her. Everywhere she went, her mom haunted her.

Sometimes it seems that things happen the way they do for a reason. Sometimes when we are so deep within the story of our own lives, we cannot see these reasons. Again, proximity distorts our perception and prevents us from gaining perspective. We can change that, though. We can practice stepping back. We don't need to move halfway around the world to do so, either, which for most of us most of the time is not feasible anyway.

There are three steps to the process of stepping back:

- Step 1: Feel the pressure.

- Step 2: Step back.

- Step 3: Relax your view.

Here's a closer look at each of these steps.

Step 1: Feel the Pressure

First of all, you need to know what too much pressure feels like. Not all pressure is bad. Often a bit of light pressure can be helpful. We don't want our blood pressure to fall too low, do we? Again, we're looking for the right amount here.

Perhaps you have seen the movie *The Horse Whisperer,* or read the book of the same title. *The Horse Whisperer* described a couple of different methods of training horses. The old method was to "break them." Often, this was done with quite tragic outcomes. A horse might be injured—or even killed—in the process. In other words, forceful pressure was applied. Pressure was exerted against the horse to try and convince the horse who was boss and how the game was going to be played. It was assumed that a good horse would comply. An unruly one? You guessed it. An unruly horse was either put down or physically abused.

The horse whisperer, however, used other methods to train horses. Now, these methods sometimes also involved pressure, but rather than being coercive, the pressure used on the horse was constant and gentle.

You have undoubtedly felt the difference between a coercive and controlling pressure and a constant gentle pressure that was there to guide you or keep you safe. In your own experience of life, you can probably reflect on situations in which you felt pressured to comply with the dictates of others. Maybe you felt emotionally blackmailed in a relationship. Maybe you were coerced by your employer to take on more work than was feasible or healthy for you.

Some forms of pressure may not be in our best interests, but we may feel like we have to comply with them anyway, for one reason or another. Other forms of pressure are constant and gentle; they guide and support us. Step 1 is *to notice the pressure you feel, and begin to learn how to tell the difference between these two types of pressure.* This way, when you feel that it is coercive pressure pushing on you from the outside (or inside), you can then go to step 2.

Step 2: Step Back

After you have registered the sensation of feeling pressured, go ahead and *find a way to step back and get some distance from whatever you feel pressured by.* It can be a mental form of stepping back—where you give yourself a little emotional space and room to breathe—or it can be that you literally need to step back, removing yourself, physically, from a specific situation or environment.

The reason you need to step back is simple: any choice you make when you are feeling under pressure is not being made under the best of circumstances, and such choices will therefore tend to be suboptimal and not be in your best interest. Odds are, in fact, that you will probably regret any decision that you make under pressure.

If we don't learn to step back after realizing we are feeling pressured, we can end up in a very reactive state that feeds a sense of powerlessness, as if we are constantly being pushed around and manipulated by others and their demands on us.

■ Megan's Story

Megan initially came to see me for an eating disorder, which she had developed as a teenager. Megan's mother was depressed and used alcohol as a means of coping. She would become emotionally and verbally abusive when she was drunk.

Megan said that she felt pressured all the time when she was a child. "I felt like I had to be perfect. I was always stressed out. I think this is why I have an eating disorder like bulimia. By throwing up, I am relieving the pressure. It's like I gorge on food until I feel this pressure inside of me building up until it becomes unbearable."

Megan was very aware of what was going on. She was the type of person who analyzed herself, often quite accurately. However, her awareness alone was not enough to stop her from enacting this same tired drama over and over again. She knew some of the reasons why she was acting out like this, but she didn't know how to alter her behavior.

Working over the course of some months, Megan started to see some results from the practice of stepping back. Over time it became easier for her to feel the pressure building slowly, instead of suddenly feeling intense pressure after overeating. "Now I notice the feelings and sensations in my stomach and throat as I am eating. I can feel the sensation of fullness building slowly," she said. "I don't need to create all of that pressure so that I can then experience that moment of relief. I can let myself feel a little pressure and how that is bearable. The result is that I am not eating as much as I used to and not feeling the need to purge."

Eventually, Megan stopped purging altogether. The result was that she was healthier, she had more energy, she felt better about herself, and she didn't have this chronic obsession to binge and purge looming over her all the time.

Like Megan, you can transform your relationship to feelings of pressure. Rather than allowing that relationship to be dictated by what happened in your childhood, you can transform it into a more mature and conscious relationship. Pressure will no longer be the enemy. The next time you feel pressure, slow down, take a step back, notice what the pressure feels like without reacting to it. Simply be aware of it without responding. Once you practice this enough, you will begin to feel differently when you are under some sort of pressure. You will be able to register it with awareness rather than seek immediate relief.

Rather than being reactive and compulsive toward the pressure/relief dynamic, you can become creative and conscious toward it. This requires relaxing your view.

Step 3: Relax Your View

When you feel pressured and stressed out, your focus can become narrow and constricted. When this happens, remember to relax your view, or *take in the whole field of physical and energetic events going on around you*, rather than obsessively and compulsively fixate on that one thing you are feeling so much pressure from.

The basis of this final step is the holistic principle that our bodies and our brains are one seamless whole. Specifically, it is based on the understanding that our brains often follow our bodies. You can learn to relax and open your perspective by relaxing your eyes and opening them to more of what is going on around you.

■ Michael's Story

When Michael came to see me, he was on the verge of serious depression. He was already down and seemed to be sliding faster and faster into a downward spiral.

"I don't know what to do anymore," he said. "I feel like I'm letting everyone down—my family at home and my employers at work. I don't even know why I try anymore. I feel like I'm going to screw it all up, and the pressure is becoming unbearable."

Michael was at his wit's end. Clearly, something needed to shift, or, he felt, "everything important" to him would "be lost." But he didn't know what needed to shift. He didn't know whether he was capable of changing; or whether he was doomed and this would be how his life played out—a tragedy waiting to happen.

Was Michael really incompetent and incapable of success in his home and work life? Or was something else going on that was causing an intense feeling of pressure? Michael needed to take a step back.

According to others around Michael, he was too hard on himself and he seemed to carry the weight of the world on his shoulders. His wife would tell him, "Honey, it's okay. No one is perfect," but it never seemed to register. According to her, Michael would beat himself up over the smallest things. This tendency had gotten worse after Michael and his wife had had their first child.

The people in Michael's life thought well of him. They thought he was a great guy. "He is so smart," his wife said. "And yes, maybe those of us around him do expect too much of him sometimes. It is just that he is so smart and such a good listener that I think people confide in him and seek out his counsel."

Clearly, all the pressure was negatively affecting him. Michael was hurting—not because those around him were insensitive and rude or because he was too damaged to deal with life. Michael was hurting because he didn't want to let anyone down. Operating on his own unrealistic assumptions about what being a good man, husband, father, friend, and employee should look like, Michael had set things up so that he could not win.

Once Michael took a step back and relaxed his view, however, he could see what was going on in his life. His posture shifted. "That's right. I put so much pressure on myself to be there for everyone, because I really do care that much for those around me. I don't want to let anyone down. It kills me when I have to choose between family and work. I love them both. It breaks my heart when I have to tell a friend I cannot meet him for lunch on Wednesday because I have a huge meeting that same day. I feel like I am a failure if I cannot do it all. I want to be there for everyone, all the time."

Who can possibly be there for everyone all of the time? The pressure Michael felt was based on his own notions of who he was and had to be, not on how things were in the real world. Michael was successful according to everyone but himself. He was a good man, father, husband, employee, and friend to all who knew him. Yet he was on the verge of collapse because he believed otherwise.

Sometimes our expectations about what we should do or be can crush us. With unrealistic expectations, we are set up to fail from the start. Whenever you feel pressure, take a step back for a better view. Ask yourself where the pressure is coming from.

When you relax your view, you can see more: of what is available to you, of what is possible, and, most of all, of what could potentially serve as a solution for you, what could be a more effective long-term response to whoever or whatever is causing your feeling of pressure.

REMOVING THE PRESSURE

We all need to take a step back, now and then. This is, perhaps, even more true for anyone who is the child of a depressed parent. Having to deal with the pressure of a parent who may have been severely depressed when we were children adds to self-expectations and a sense of burden that we may end up having throughout our lives. Learning how to deal better with the pressure that comes with the territory can give us a very helpful skill.

It may take a little time to get the hang of stepping back. After all, when we are feeling pressured, it seems like we have neither the time nor the space to do anything other than wrestle with whatever is impinging upon us so heavily. It can take some practice to notice the way pressure comes upon you—the way it builds, the way it feels, the way it mounts. But once you begin to learn how to step back, and then start to see the beneficial impact it has on your relationships with others and on your own well-being, you will become fully convinced that not forcing things—including yourself—to be other than what they are is always the best path to long-term health and happiness.

KEY POINTS

- Being too close to whatever we are attempting to see is one of the greatest obstacles to effectively understanding what is going on in any given circumstance.

- Stepping back is a very useful skill for gaining better perspective, even if it feels counterintuitive at times.

- The more you feel pressured, the less you are giving yourself the room you need to grow to your full potential. When you are feeling pressured, it is time to take a step back.

- Stepping back can give you the space to breathe more freely and the room to spread and find your own wings in life. So practice feeling the pressure, stepping back, and relaxing your view; take a step back and feel yourself beginning to expand. That is what your true self is and feels like.

CHAPTER 10

Finding the Silver Linings in Parental Depression

Here you are, then. You have accomplished so much. You have looked back to the roots of your childhood and the possibility that one or both of your parents may have been depressed. You have explored how such depression cannot help but touch you deeply—both in terms of the relationship you have with yourself and the relationships you have with others. You have learned new ideas and begun to put into practice skills that will give you both new insight into your past and new ways of approaching your life today. This chapter will take you one step further to bring you even greater peace with your past.

When we are struggling—especially in our healing journey—it is sometimes impossible to see how we've benefited from what's happened in our lives. Yet, this chapter will argue, perhaps there are silver linings in store.

ART IMITATES LIFE

In the recent film *Silver Linings Playbook*, Pat Solitano Jr. (Bradley Cooper) is released from a mental institution into his parents' custody. He had been sentenced to a stay in the mental institution by court order, after having been diagnosed with bipolar disorder. Had it not been for the court order, he would have gone to jail for having severely beaten his wife's lover.

Like all great dramas, this movie holds in store many pleasant (and some unpleasant) surprises. There is dramatic tension. Things are not always what they seem. Something "bad" can lead to something good. For instance, Pat realized that the woman he thought he wanted was not in the end who he really wanted. What is first judged as a tragedy can turn into a triumph. These kinds of twists and turns of plot are not just for the movies, though. Life can be just as dramatic sometimes. Some of the best things in our lives come from its toughest moments.

We don't always know and appreciate the reality of dramatic tension and resolution when it is staring us in the face. Again, it seems we often have neither the time nor the distance necessary for perspective. When we are in the throes of drama, it feels like we may become undone, or may drown, or that our whole life may unravel. We become totally immersed—never knowing what the next scene holds—and can easily forget that it might actually be wonderful and amazing.

This brings to mind another great movie in which art imitates life. In *It's a Wonderful Life*, George Bailey (Jimmy Stewart) begins to contemplate suicide when he sees no way out of an impossible situation. He is being framed for bank fraud by Mr. Potter, an evil businessman, real estate developer, and banker. In a drunken state, George crashes his car into a tree. Then he walks to a bridge where he prepares to jump, shouting out the words to Heaven, "I wish I had never been born."

Then, just as George is about to take his life, his guardian angel, Clarence, appears and throws himself into the river, forcing George to momentarily forget about himself and rescue him. Clarence then proceeds to show George what his life would have been like had he never been born. With the help of some perspective—provided from the view granted him by his guardian angel—George Bailey realizes that life would not be so wonderful without him. All of the people he loves and cares about would experience greater suffering without him in their lives.

The perspective provided to George allows him to see that he's had a wonderful life. Even with great challenges, life can indeed be wonderful.

SHIFTING YOUR PERSPECTIVE

Chapter 9 focused on teaching you how to step back from your experience to get a broader view. This skill is instrumental in allowing for a shift in perspective. How crucial this process is cannot be overstated at this point in your journey toward healing. Shifting your perspective will not alter the actual events of your history, but it will allow you to perceive those events in a different light. The visualization in this exercise will help to illuminate what a mere shift in your perspective can accomplish.

Exercise: Shifting Your Perspective

Imagine you are leaning against a large tree. On the other side of the tree, the sun shines brightly. As you stand with your back to the tree, your view is drawn to the shadows cast by the tree blocking the sun's light. Now think about this: What you see is a bit darker than maybe what truly is. It is not that the shadows are an illusion. It is just that they are not the whole story. If you keep leaning with your back against the tree this way, you might assume that is all there is: a tree with a large shadow. But what if you move to a different side of the tree? What happens then? Might you suddenly have a very different view of the landscape? You might still see the shadow, out of the corner of your eye, but you will also see a landscape filled with sunlight.

The same sort of process happens in our healing. When we are seeing only the shadows and our back is up against the tree of our personal life history, the terrain we are living in can appear pretty bleak. So long as we remain there, and there is no shift in our perspective, we may believe that what we are seeing is the whole truth. But we would be missing out, wouldn't we?

To reiterate: The shadow side of our lives is not untrue; it is not an illusion. The dark and challenging things that have happened to us did, in fact, happen to us. But if we see only the darkness of our personal history, then we will miss out on the light of life itself.

Moving Out of the Shadows

Hopefully this book has helped you find ways to move out of the shadows of your parent's depression. Feeling doomed to a life in the shadows is not helpful. And you are not doomed. No one should suffer needlessly because they haven't found out or heard about the fact that there is a way out, or that there are other options available.

Again, we can't change the facts about what happened. The events that took place *did* take place, and parental depression can have a dramatic impact on children. Furthermore, real healing is not about telling ourselves it's okay when it clearly was not at times. Real healing is not about manufacturing comfortable illusions to compensate for uncomfortable truths. Real healing is about accepting the reality of what has happened and then discovering creative and uplifting—rather than reactive and deadening—ways to deal with your heritage and inheritance.

Real healing comes when you move out of the shadows and onto the other side of the tree of life, where the sun shines brightly. After all, even a shadow isn't possible without the sun. It is in that light alone that you have the potential to discover the treasure that can be mined from your most challenging experiences. Yes, that's right—there is treasure to be mined in all that you have wished to be free from. Like George Bailey's discovery in *It's a Wonderful Life* and Pat Solitano's realization in *Silver Linings Playbook*, the real treasure is right under our noses.

Suspending Your Disbelief

Please consider the possibility that your parent's depression was not only a curse but also a blessing. Consider the possibility that there is something wonderful that is a part of you that others will not have—ever!—precisely because they did not have the experiences that you had as a child of a depressed parent. Put differently, there are no doubt some silver linings in your own life's playbook.

You may or may not agree with this—yet. Or perhaps, by now, you are starting to get a glimmer of what some of these silver linings may be. Maybe you are realizing how much you have learned to care about others. Maybe you are starting to appreciate how sensitive you are, because you had to be so attuned to your parent's condition as a child. Maybe you are beginning to realize that, while your experience as a child was not idyllic, it was rich and fertile ground for some amazing discoveries about yourself that others without this kind of life history can never know. Maybe it is not so far-fetched to understand that the whole story of your parent's depression does not exist only on the shadow side of the tree.

If this is not the case, however, and you still feel any hesitation or reluctance at this point, I want to remind you that I, too, was a child of a depressed parent. I know what it is like. I have walked the hallowed grounds of depression and been on both sides of the equation and both sides of the tree. I was the child wondering what was wrong with my parent and also the depressed parent who suffered greatly with postpartum depression. This is not theoretical territory for me. This is personal and intimate.

So yes, I know all about this, personally. I was once full of doubt and skepticism. I was the one who was drenched in disbelief anytime someone tried to remind me of what might be a more positive perspective than the one I had. Many clients, as well, have shared that sense of disbelief, only to eventually discover that, yes, there are silver linings in the darkest of life's clouds, and light in the most terrifying of storms.

You may be asking, "How can anything positive come from what I lost—the best part of my childhood—or was forced to suffer with? How can anyone be so callous as to suggest that what happened to me was a good thing?"

For starters, clearly it does not feel good when anyone you know becomes depressed, let alone if it is your parent. What you can do, though, is take what you experienced as suffering and transform it. No one can go back in time and give us a parent who was not depressed. But again, your perception of what happened can certainly change.

This book has given you some new ways to examine your past experience and some new skills, including SCARS and buying yourself time, to help you in the present. The goal has been to take the edge off of any suffering that you may currently be experiencing and—maybe, just maybe—help you discover some new ways to make peace with your past.

FINDING THE SILVER LININGS

While the unique journey that you are on will likely reveal silver linings that are specific to you and apply to your particular experience, you may have other experiences in common with others. A few of these experiences appear with such frequency—they emerge in the awareness of so many who are recovering from the childhood wounds of having a depressed parent—that they deserve special mention here.

Forgiveness

Often, experiences of blame, regret, and shame can be associated with remembering our parents and their depression. Feelings of having lost out on certain aspects of our childhood may predominate. Maybe we had to grow up too fast. Maybe we did not have the carefree childhood that we wished we could have had. All of this can perpetuate feelings of blame, shame, and regret.

Eventually, though, we find ourselves moving into a softer place in our lives. Maybe one day we can come to the realization that our parent suffered greatly, too. Usually there was no malice or intent to harm us. Typically, depressed mothers and fathers are not out to get us. Quite the contrary, depressed parents often go overboard trying to protect their children from their depression; they love their children very much and try as hard as they can to avoid hurting them. It may not be easy to acknowledge this, at first. However, as the roots of our own healing deepen, we cannot help but move to a place of forgiveness on our journey. It is as inevitable for us as it was for Susie.

■ Susie's Story Continued

Susie had struggled in her relationship with her mother and her controlling ways (see chapter 7). Eventually, it became so bad that Susie told her mom that she would have to find other accommodations when she came to town to visit Susie and her family. This led to some awkwardness and tension between them. It also, eventually, made for much more honest and open communication. Susie became firmer and more direct with her mother, and her mother, in contrast, became softer and much more open and receptive to what Susie wanted and needed.

The real breakthrough, however, came when Susie told her mom that she forgave her: "I told her that I didn't blame her for being who she was. She always had to be in control and keep everything together. I don't think she knew how to be any different. She saw it as her way to love and support me. All of that unasked-for advice and help was just her being a mom. She really had no idea how it affected me. I know my telling her was a shock at first. I know it also hurt her. But I also give her a lot of credit. She didn't curse me or shut down completely. Yes, there were moments when communication between us would break down, and we needed to take a step back from one another. Ultimately, though, our love and care prevailed, and we found ways of honoring each other without stepping on each other's toes.

"I know it really helped her when I told her, 'Mom, I don't blame you. It was not your fault. Things are different now and I am not a child—even if I will always be your baby. We are both growing and discovering how to better relate and communicate with each other. I forgive you, and I hope you forgive me too.' I know it helped me."

Susie told her mom that she didn't harbor any ill will or antagonistic feelings toward her. For Susie and her mom, the air had finally been cleared. Communication could be more forthright, honest, and direct, without either of them feeling like they were under attack. This didn't mean that their challenges in communicating went away entirely.

We always will have moments where we slip up or fall into the behaviors and attitudes of the past. But this also means that we have another opportunity to both ask for—and offer to those around us—the blessing and gift that is forgiveness.

Compassion

Might compassion be a potential silver lining that you can discover in the dark clouds of the past? As the child of a depressed parent, it's very likely that you have developed an ongoing compassionate response to the suffering of others. You learned it as a child through your direct and intimate awareness of your parent's ongoing suffering.

What child wants his parent or parents to suffer? What child is not plagued by the ongoing question of a parent's suffering? The stories of most adult children of the depressed reveal that, as children, they always exhibited a proclivity to want to help their parents. If that is not an indication of the presence of real compassion, then I don't know what is.

■ Jacob's Story Continued

You might recall Jacob's story from chapter 7. Jacob's mother was in and out of mental-health institutions much of his childhood. You may also recall how accommodating Jacob was in doing everything he could to avoid disrupting or upsetting his mother when she was at home. Obviously, this ended up creating some issues for Jacob later in his adult relationships with women. He had issues with setting personal boundaries in intimate relationships and honestly stating his own needs. Yet, as Jacob retold his experience of being a child, the love he felt for his mother was evident.

"I always wanted her to be happy," he said. "I remember doing everything I could to make sure that I was quiet in the house when I came home from school. I also never invited friends over. At the time, it was what I wanted to do. I loved my mom. Even if she was not well, she was still my mom. I would have done anything for her when I was a kid."

Most of us would do anything. Anything at all. The love of our parents runs so very, very deep. Within this love, there is often evidence of compassion—specifically, the desire or wish to alleviate the suffering of our parents. It is, perhaps, why children of the depressed end up being stand-in caregivers for their parents. As adults, this compassion is a gift. Not everyone has it, but as children of the depressed, we often do.

Gratitude

Much of this book has been devoted to helping you find meaning and make sense out of the events that have happened in your life. In many ways, this is what makes healing possible. Meaning and significance are not givens. If meaning were a given, and you were truly cursed because you were a child of the depressed, then there would be no point in attempting to offer hope and healing. Fortunately, that is not the case.

The meaning that events have for us is not something we can read about in a book or be handed by others. What your parent's depression means for you is, in the final analysis, ultimately up to you—and only you. How I construct and create what my parent's depression has meant for me in my life is an act of my own choosing, just as the meaning you give to your own upbringing is an act of your own choosing. Even choosing not to find meaning in the events of your life is an act, or a choice, you can make. There's no obligation to find meaning, but there is an opportunity.

■ Janice's Story Continued

As a young woman, Janice sacrificed her life, love, and career in Europe to return home to care for her father after her mother's passing (see chapter 8). For Janice, the turning point in her recovery was recognizing what those many years of struggle had brought her. She found a new meaning in the events of her life, as she explained.

"For nearly a decade, I was depressed myself, feeling like I gave up everything for my family. I was often resentful and bitter, too. Yes, I loved my dad and wanted to be there for him as much as I could, but I was also sad and tragically bereft of any hope that I would ever have my own life again. I felt like I had sacrificed my one and only chance at a happy existence." But then, her perspective shifted.

"I see it all quite differently now. Yes, I did give up a lot. I was also given a lot, too. When I came home, I was not able to avoid my upbringing anymore. I couldn't just run away to Europe. I realize now that I was carrying this heaviness in my heart the whole time. I didn't truly get away from it while I was in Europe. It was always inside of me."

Janice started painting: "I felt all of this stuff inside of me that wanted to come out. All of these images and colors were living inside of me. I am convinced that if I had stayed in Europe, I would be curating the art of others and not giving birth to my own. The irony is that what I felt was the worst thing that could have ever happened to me has turned out to be one of the best. If I had not come home and felt trapped here, I doubt the artist I was meant to be would have ever been awakened. I am so, so very grateful for what all of this has shown me and helped give birth to. It wasn't easy, by any means. But now I know I had to go through that hell to arrive at where I am today."

Janice exhibits her paintings at a community art gallery that's near where she lives. Her father is now in an assisted living facility not far away. She volunteers in the local schools helping children discover their own inner artists. Her life has taken unexpected twists and turns. "My life didn't go the way I expected it to. Not even the way I wanted it to! But I wouldn't change a thing. It's a life that is perfect for me, and perfectly mine."

We can look at our lives in so many different ways—some positive, some less so. As a child of the depressed, you had a unique and difficult experience that was no one else's. It shaped who you are, just as, by shifting your perspective on events, you can shape your life to come.

FINAL THOUGHTS

Life is truly full of surprises. Some pleasant. Some that feel tragic and are certainly unexpected. There are chance meetings that turn into lifelong friendships or loves. There are unforeseen challenges that force us to draw on reserves of strength and stamina that maybe we never knew we possessed. There are heartbreaks and breakthroughs. There are quantum leaps and leaps of faith.

My wish for you, if you are a child of the depressed, is that whatever childhood wounds you may still possess turn into well-healed scars that are beloved because they hold an amazing story or that serve as a reminder of what has touched you so deeply. That your scars become stories that heal and touch, uplift, and inspire not only you but those around you.

My hope is that you come to a place where you can wear your scars proudly and are unafraid to share the stories that live within those scars. After all, what are scars but the memory of a wound and of a healing that has already occurred? What happened during those years that you lived with a depressed parent does not and should not define who you are in total. But it certainly can add to your wholeness in important and wonderfully enriching ways.

References

American Psychiatric Association. 2013. *Diagnostic and Statistical Manual of Mental Disorders (DSM-V)*. 5th ed. Washington, DC: American Psychiatric Association.

Bateson, G. 1971. "The Cybernetics of Self: A Theory of Alcoholism," *Psychiatry* 34: 1.

Bowlby, J. 1969. *Attachment and Loss*. Vol. 1. New York: Penguin Books.

National Institute of Mental Health. 2013. "Signs and Symptoms of Depression." http://www.nimh.nih.gov/health/topics/depres sion/men-and-depression/signs-and-symptoms-of-depression /index.shtml

Shoshana S. Bennett, PhD, is a pioneer in the field of parental depression and its effects on children. A clinical psychologist and media expert, Bennett has inspired and transformed countless lives worldwide through her radio shows, books, and videos. She is the creator of the free app *PPD Gone!*; author of several books, including *Pregnant on Prozac* and *Postpartum Depression for Dummies*; and a past president of Postpartum Support International. Bennett has trained thousands of medical, mental health, and newborn care professionals on the topic of parental depression, providing common-sense tools to overcome these conditions and protect children. To find out more, visit www .drshosh.com.

Foreword writer **Nelson Branco, MD**, is a practicing pediatrician in Marin County, CA. He is the managing partner of Tamalpais Pediatrics, and has worked in varied settings providing primary care to children and teens over the past two decades.

FROM OUR PUBLISHER—

As the publisher at New Harbinger and a clinical psychologist since 1978, I know that emotional problems are best helped with evidence-based therapies. These are the treatments derived from scientific research (randomized controlled trials) that show what works. Whether these treatments are delivered by trained clinicians or found in a self-help book, they are designed to provide you with proven strategies to overcome your problem.

Therapies that aren't evidence-based—whether offered by clinicians or in books—are much less likely to help. In fact, therapies that aren't guided by science may not help you at all. That's why this New Harbinger book is based on scientific evidence that the treatment can relieve emotional pain.

This is important: if this book isn't enough, and you need the help of a skilled therapist, use the following resources to find a clinician trained in the evidence-based protocols appropriate for your problem. And if you need more support—a community that understands what you're going through and can show you ways to cope—resources for that are provided below, as well.

Real help is available for the problems you have been struggling with. The skills you can learn from evidence-based therapies will change your life.

Matthew McKay, PhD
Publisher, New Harbinger Publications

If you need a therapist, the following organization can help you find a therapist trained in cognitive behavioral therapy (CBT).

The Association for Behavioral & Cognitive Therapies (ABCT) Find-a-Therapist service offers a list of therapists schooled in CBT techniques. Therapists listed are licensed professionals who have met the membership requirements of ABCT and who have chosen to appear in the directory.

Please visit www.abct.org and click on *Find a Therapist*.

For additional support for patients, family, and friends, please contact the following:

Anxiety and Depression Association of American (ADAA) **visit www.adaa.org**

Depression and Bipolar Support Alliance (DBSA) **visit www.dbsalliance.org**

National Alliance on Mental Illness (NAMI) **visit www.nami.org**

National Suicide Prevention Lifeline **Call 24 hours a day 1-800-273-TALK (8255) or visit suicidepreventionlifeline.org**